Pr

The Je

"*The Jesus Climb* should prove a powerful tool for educators and pastors seeking to connect discipleship to spiritual awakening in the lives of those they lead. I trust it will find a wide audience for promoting authentic discipleship in a new generation."

—**David S. Medders,** Executive Vice President, The Association of Biblical Higher Education

"What a delightful read. As a pastoral psychotherapist I am constantly looking for resources that aid my client's journey of self-awareness and spiritual growth. Dr. Stratton's book is a wonderful guide to help unearth the things deep within us. His insightful metaphors and astute biblical wisdom forge a developmental path toward the heights of understanding how becoming a disciple of Christ enables us to become the fullest version of the person God intended us to be."

—**John Mokkosian,** Cofounder of The New England Pastoral Institute

"*The Jesus Climb* has the potential to revolutionize the life of an individual, family, and church by inviting us into a rigorous and ravishing vision for following Jesus and how we can genuinely shine his beautiful light in the world. Gary connects so easily with students—and other listeners—with the kind of substance, meaning, and depth in our Christian faith that is life-changing. *The Jesus Climb* is just an extension of Gary—and a critical one for anyone who really wants to find joy, hope, and love increasing in measure as we say yes to the hard but beautiful work of following Jesus."

—**Peter B. Kapsner,** PhD, Talk Show Host, Deeper Magic Media, Theology Professor, Northwestern University St Paul

"Gary Stratton shines a light on the spiritual journey Jesus crafted for his disciples. Rich in design, centered on Scripture, and full of inspiring examples and transformational application, *The Jesus Climb* engages the heart and the mind from start to finish."

—**Scott Reitz,** PhD, Associate Professor of Intercultural Studies and Director of Global Service Learning and First-Year Studies, Alliance University

"The discipleship concepts in *The Jesus Climb* transformed my life as a student. Now they are transforming the lives of the students in my classroom. I trust you too will grow as you learn to follow our Lord Jesus as your Teacher and to live out Jesus's teachings in every area of your life."

—**Kirk McClelland,** EdD, Professor of Service Learning, Director of First-Year Studies, Johnson University

"*The Jesus Climb* brilliantly provides young adults with a pathway for taking responsibility for their faith formation. Stratton skillfully conceived these truly timeless concepts that resonate with each generation."

—**Dr. Mark Cannister,** Professor of Christian Ministries, Gordon College

"*The Jesus Climb* is a great tool to begin with the end in mind as we work to make lifelong followers of Jesus. Staff, student leaders, college students, and new believers will find great inspiration in this book."

—**Nathaniel and Kendra Williams,** Campus Life Gold Country, Youth for Christ, USA

"This book beautifully and practically unpacks what it means to climb the mountain of life as a *disciple* of Jesus Christ. Gary provides insights and illustrations to explain and teach the upward and downward journey as a disciple of Christ—a personal and encountering journey experienced in the context of a spiritual community."

—**Rev. Dr. Jonathan Lee,** President of Streamside Ministry

"*The Jesus Climb* is written for those wishing to discover what it means to be true followers of Jesus rather than mere advocates of Christianity. Cleverly woven as a challenging climb for those seeking intimacy with God, it is practical, honest, and frank. Laced with human interest stories for illustration, the book examines what it means to surrender to the One who first loved us, embody his teaching, and join the community he is creating."

—**Richard L. Gathro,** EdD, International Arts & Education Traveler, US Liaison Officer, Kellogg College, Oxford

"Gary provides a fresh, accessible mnemonic metaphor for Christian formation. Like a Sherpa guiding seekers on Mt. Everest to the top and back, he shares hard-earned wisdom from his faith journey to guide God-seekers not only to a summit but on a long-term expedition to love God, self, and neighbor. Complete with practical exercises, the book is an essential resource for all who may have experienced a revival in their lives and wonder what's next."

—**Jodi L. Porter,** EdD, Director of Education for Ministry Innovation, Acadia Divinity College

"I firmly believe God has used Dr. Stratton to bring to the Body of Christ a word of hope, restoration, realignment, and direction through his insightful references and personal anecdotes in this compelling book. A catalyst for revival, *The Jesus Climb* has catapulted my faith to 'summit high' levels by drawing me into a deeper understanding of the power of intimacy through discipleship."

—**Carla Debbie Alleyne,** playwright and screenwriter

"Dr. Stratton produces a relatable, intentional model for those on their discipleship journey who desire to learn more about Jesus and what it looks like to truly follow him. Through personal stories and the metaphor of a 'climb,' he shows students how to both learn more about God through commitment to him and grow deeper in intimacy with Christ."

—**Hannah Miller,** undergraduate senior, Johnson University

"With a conversational tone and accessible metaphors and examples, Gary presents an intriguing and inspirational take on being a better teacher, student, and disciple—and how those three intertwine."

—**Sheryl J. Anderson,** writer/producer, *Sweet Magnolias, Charmed*

"*The Jesus Climb* provides a necessary and insightful perspective on how vital discipleship is in the life of Jesus followers no matter where they are in their faith journey. The book is a refreshing yet practical model for living out one's faith with intention and deep commitment to God and God's people."

—**Dr. Dametraus L. Jaggers,** Pastor and Church Planter of City Church Clarksville

"Each chapter presents biblical teaching on being disciples of Jesus, set within the illuminating context of wisdom from Everest climbers. Along the way we meet Christian role models whose life journeys can inspire and encourage us to keep climbing with Jesus. I highly commend this readable, engaging, and biblically sound manual for growth into Jesus."

—**Klaus Issler,** PhD, Emeritus Professor of Educational Studies and Theology, author of *Living into the Life of Jesus*

"Combining gripping tales of Mt. Everest with stories of faithful disciples over the centuries, Gary Stratton masterfully weaves together a guide for anyone attempting to live like the Rabbi Jesus taught. Practical as well as inspirational, this book is the discipleship guide I've been searching for as I continue to make following Jesus part of my daily rhythm of life."

—**Melissa Chang,** Vice Chair and Founder of DemandScience

"A brilliant navigation of Christianity in the modern world using a comparison model that crosses generations: summiting Mt. Everest. With Gary as your expedition guide, this is a must-read for those looking to take the next step in their spiritual journey."

—**Leslie Stratton,** 2-time World Championship, 4-time European Championship, and World Cup Skeleton Athlete

"*The Jesus Climb* is a thought-provoking guide for anyone seeking to understand what Jesus says about true discipleship. Gary Stratton doesn't just talk the talk; he embodies it.

—**Sandra Uwiringiyimana,** Human Rights Advocate, author of *How Dare the Sunrise*

"Gary is a trustworthy Sherpa guiding you on the journey up and down the Mt. Everest of discipleship. This book is a trail guide you can follow as you lead others in this process. I was deeply encouraged by the warmth and wisdom of Gary's words to continue growing closer to Jesus by discipling others."

—**James W. Shores,** PhD, Professor of Communication, Asbury University

"This book will lead people to not only a more truthful experience of Jesus but also a truthful expression of him."

—**Mike Friesen,** Therapist and Theologian

"Stratton's writing is compelling and intensely practical. He provides an abundance of actionable advice for next steps for every disciple's spiritual formation. And he does this with humility and grace, as someone who has spent a lifetime learning how to navigate the exhilarating and demanding terrain of the embodied Christ life."

—**Rob Blackaby,** President, Canadian Baptist Theological Seminary and College

"Ascending to the summit and then descending to the base of a mountain is exhilarating. Doing so metaphorically as a student ascending the mountain of life, lovingly following Jesus, and then descending the same toward humble maturity is even more meaningful. This is the expedition Stratton invites us to consider, one step at a time, toward ever-increasing spiritual maturity."

—**Stephen A. Macchia,** Founder and President, Leadership Transformations; Director, Pierce Center at Gordon-Conwell Theological Seminary; author of *The Discerning Life, Broken and Whole,* and *Becoming a Healthy Church*

"Stratton provides a compelling, stimulating narrative on how to pursue the seemingly insurmountable summit of true Christian faith, particularly for those sliding down the slope of doubt or the frustration of anemic Christianity."

—**Laurel Bunker,** Principal Consultant, The Boncoeur Collaborative

"Gary Stratton harnesses personal stories, scriptural insight, spiritual practices, and a diverse cloud of witnesses to clarify Christ's command to 'Follow me.' Stratton's easy and accessible writing style enhances his practical and patient approach to becoming a disciple. *The Jesus Climb* will enrich Christians of every age, calling all generations to partner with the Spirit to ascend and descend the mountain of Christ that oddly resembles Calvary and a cross."

—**Shane J. Wood,** Professor of New Testament & Its Origins, Ozark Christian College; author of *Between Two Trees*

"*The Jesus Climb* is not some mere sketch of an imagined land but contains proven truths and hard-won insights from one who knows the territory well. Stratton is a trustworthy guide to the adventurous and life-shaping path of becoming a disciple of Jesus. *The Jesus Climb* is a practical, biblical guidebook for all who desire to follow Jesus, no matter where they are on their pilgrimage."

—**Rev. Gregory W. Carmer,** PhD, Pastor, Church in the Cove, Beverly, MA

"There's something about a mountain: the lure, the call, the beauty, the challenge. There's something about this book: its invitation to climb toward Jesus, its brilliant mnemonics device (D.I.S.C.I.P.L.E.), its rich historical connections, its clarion call to risk it all. Climb on!"

—**Daniel Curran,** Senior Campus Minister, Berkeley Cru

"Gary Stratton has long been committed to strengthening the faith of his students at their most vulnerable moments—not just sustaining their faith but nurturing it for the challenges ahead. *The Jesus Climb* seeks to bolster the spiritual 'red cell count' for the long ascent. Rooted in personal anecdotes and hard questions, the book offers practical counsel and inspiration, always alert to the ways Jesus taught and walked the trail before us."

—**Mark Sargent,** Senior Fellow, Council for Christian Colleges and Universities

"Gary Stratton calls us to the adventure of discipleship and packs his guidebook for spiritual 'mountaineers' with creative practices, fresh readings of Scripture, and loads of inspiring stories. Get ready to follow Christ as the ultimate Sherpa and develop the strength needed to ascend with him to the heights."

—**Gwenfair Walters Adams,** PhD, Professor of Church History and Spiritual Formation, Chair, Division of Christian Thought, Director of Spiritual Formation Studies, Gordon-Conwell Theological Seminary

"This is not a pop-out trivial treatment of discipleship. Gary's writing is informed by solid scholarship, yet it is not pedantic. It is personal, engaging, realistic, and helpful in the climb and adventure of following Jesus in this world. This is a wonderful book for students, and some of us who are not so young, who are hoping for guidance in mapping out their lives as it is centered in discipleship to Jesus."

—**Michael J. Wilkins,** PhD, Distinguished Professor Emeritus of New Testament Language and Literature, Talbot School of Theology, Biola University; author of *Following the Master*

"Gary's creativity amazes me, and I found myself unable to put the book down! I trust him, and I trust you too will experience the beauty of Jesus and his gospel in unexpected and ever-unfolding ways on the journey of *The Jesus Climb!*"

—**Tim Savaloja,** Executive Coach, author of *Thoughts of God*

"Summitting Mt. Everest is for the committed and courageous few who train and train. This is just the opposite of how student discipleship training often works in a culture that demands a 'quick fix' with a high priority on 'having fun.' Following Christ is the highest of aspirations and demands the best of us. Stratton in clear, inspiring, and practical ways guides students on the journey of a robust relationship with Jesus Christ."

—**Dr. MaryKate Morse,** PhD, Professor of Leadership and Spiritual Formation, Portland Seminary; author of *Lifelong Leadership*

"Gary Stratton clearly understands the struggle of discipleship. He knows what it's like to clamber toward the summit of authentic spirituality, mature Christianity (marked by a genuine love for God and those around us). The life he commends involves sacrifice and suffering but leads to profound joy, peace, and belonging."

—**Douglas A. Sweeney,** Dean, Beeson Divinity School, Samford University; author of *The Substance of Our Faith*

"Stratton's book is full of stories, ideas, and practices to inspire and equip you for the greatest expedition of all: becoming mature in Christ. Lace up your climbing boots, grab your ice axe and belay, pack your ropes, and get ready for the climb—*The Jesus Climb,* that is."

—**Dr. Michael Frost,** Founding Director of the Tinsley Institute, Morling College; author of *The Shaping of Things to Come, Mission Is the Shape of Water,* and *ReJesus*

"Written in both a reflective and captivating style, *The Jesus Climb* beautifully portrays the intricate path of authentic discipleship. Infused with real-life stories of biblical, historical, and present-day disciples, *The Jesus Climb* offers a compelling vision of what it means to live a life fully aligned with Jesus."

—**Alan Hirsch,** award-winning author, including *The Forgotten Ways*; Founder of Movement Leaders Collective and Forge Missional Training Network

"Built around Mallory's epic Mt. Everest adventure, Gary's page-turner distills the Great Tradition's timeless wisdom on spiritual formation into eight clear stages through which every Jesus follower must pass as they pursue spiritual maturity. Conversational, honest, fast-paced, and timely, *The Jesus Climb* is the first book I'll reach for when encouraging new spiritual climbers just arriving in base camp."

—**Douglas Banister,** Knoxville Leadership Foundation, author of *The Word and Power Church* and *The Sacred Quest*

"Gary Stratton takes us on an exhilarating expedition up the spiritual Everest, offering profound insights and invaluable guidance for anyone seeking a deeper connection with Jesus. Stratton's eloquent writing, spiritual insight, and profound analogies will inspire you to embark on your own spiritual ascent, equipped with the wisdom and faith to conquer the highest peaks of your faith journey. Whether you're at base camp or already well on your way, this book will guide you toward the summit of an enriching and transformative relationship with Jesus."

—**Cara Smith,** Executive Director, The Pure Incubation Foundation

"Gary's ability to weave biblical, historical, and personal stories into the narrative arc of a parable comparing climbing the world's tallest mountain with following Jesus's greatest commandment is as captivating as any Hollywood production."

—**Brian Bird,** Executive Producer/writer, *When Calls the Heart* and *Captive*; writer, *Not Easily Broken* and *The Case for Christ*

"*The Jesus Climb* is a gift in both theory and practice in a world so desperately broken and in need of the restorative power of Jesus. It is Gary's relentless and continuing pursuit of the ways of Jesus compounded with an abundance of experiences and encounters with students, young and old alike, that makes this book an indispensable guide on all our climbs."

—**Mark Nelson,** Executive Director of Three Rivers Collaborative; coauthor of *Reframation*

"Suspend reality for a moment and imagine yourself in the multiverse. Instead of the church-verse with its services, sermons, and offering plates, *The Jesus Climb* will take you into a 'Jesus college'-verse. In this alternative reality you will gain a fresh look at the person of Jesus—who he is and who he is inviting you to become: *his* student, *his* disciple."

—**Mike Johnson,** Pastor of Discipleship and Learning, Impact Church; author of *Impact Darkness with Light*

"I've always known Gary to be kind, earnest, and funny, and I have no doubt you will find *The Jesus Climb* to be at least two of those things, maybe even all three."

—**Pete Holmes,** Comedian, writer, actor, Producer, *The Pete Holmes Show* (TNT), *Crashing* (HBO), *How We Roll* (CBS), *You Made It Weird* (podcast)

"After decades of working with hundreds of churches worldwide, I've discovered the reason Christianity is virtually disappearing isn't because of poor marketing, politics, or lack of relevance. The problem is the *lack of discipleship*. We simply aren't living the life God has called us to live, and as a result, we're making little to no impact on today's culture. But now, Stratton has given us a roadmap. Simply put, it's the key to turning everything around."

—**Phil Cooke,** PhD, Filmmaker, writer, and author of *The Way Back*

"Beautiful in its simplicity, *The Jesus Climb* is embedded with unforgettable metaphors, riveting stories, and a relaxed honesty—all in service of a discipleship that is centered on a deepening intimacy with Jesus. It will inspire you, then help you live into that inspiration."

—**Rick Lawrence,** Executive Director of Vibrant Faith, author of *Editing Jesus, The Jesus-Centered Life,* and *Jesus-Centered Daily*

"Stratton's vulnerability and wisdom in *The Jesus Climb* won my heart and mind. As I followed his central metaphor of climbing and descending Mt. Everest, I found myself longing to follow Jesus more deeply and faithfully from one Expedition Camp to the next. I wholeheartedly recommend this spiritual climbing guide to students of all ages."

—**Doug Clark,** National Field Director, The National Network of Youth Ministry

"*The Jesus Climb* supplies readers with foundational approaches for following Jesus, enduring in their faith through all of life, and embodying Jesus's teachings within their lived context. Framing this journey with parallels to climbing Mt. Everest, Stratton establishes his approach with a memorable acronym (D.I.S.C.I.P.L.E.) and bolsters it with real-life stories filled with wisdom for following Jesus as a generative journey rather than a list of prescribed steps."

—**Andrew M. Frazier,** EdD, Vice President for Student Life at Johnson University

"Gary Stratton is a gifted communicator who will inform you, challenge you, coach you, and lead you from wherever you are to help you grow as a disciple of Jesus."

—**Clinton E. Arnold,** Research Professor of New Testament, Talbot School of Theology (Biola University)

"*The Jesus Climb* is designed to assist disciples and disciplers in the 'climb' that is our spiritual journey. The personal examples and rich resources provide the reader with a framework to up their discipleship game. Jesus modeled discipleship producing powerful results that ultimately changed the world. Take the time to read this book—you won't be the same!"

—**Philip Dearborn,** President of the Association for Biblical Higher Education

THE JESUS CLIMB

JOURNEYING FROM STUDENT TO DISCIPLE

GARY DAVID STRATTON

LEAFWOOD
PUBLISHERS
an imprint of Abilene Christian University Press

THE JESUS CLIMB
Journeying from Student to Disciple

LEAFWOOD
P U B L I S H E R S
an imprint of Abilene Christian University Press

Copyright © 2024 by Gary Stratton

ISBN 978-1-68426-112-3 | LCCN 2023024693

Printed in the United States of America

Scripture quotations, unless otherwise noted, are from the Holy Bible, New International Version®, NIV®. Copyright © 1973, 1978, 1984, 2011 by Biblica, Inc.™ Used by permission of Zondervan. All rights reserved worldwide.

Scripture quotations noted GDS are translated by the author, Gary D. Stratton.

Scripture quotations noted *The Message* taken from *The Message*. Copyright © 1993, 1994, 1995, 1996, 2000, 2001, 2002. Used by permission of NavPress Publishing Group.

LIBRARY OF CONGRESS CATALOGING-IN-PUBLICATION DATA
Names: Stratton, Gary David, author.
Title: The Jesus climb : journeying from student to disciple / Gary David Stratton.
Description: Abilene, Texas : Leafwood Publishers, [2024] | Includes bibliographical references.
Identifiers: LCCN 2023024693 | ISBN 9781684261123 | ISBN 9781684268924 (ebook)
Subjects: LCSH: Christian life. | Followership.
Classification: LCC BV4501.3 .S7747 2024 | DDC 248.4—dc23/eng/20231206
LC record available at https://lccn.loc.gov/2023024693

Cover design by Faceout
Interior text design by Sandy Armstrong, Strong Design

Leafwood Publishers is an imprint of Abilene Christian University Press.
ACU Box 29138
Abilene, Texas 79699

1-877-816-4455
www.leafwoodpublishers.com

24 25 26 27 28 29 30 // 7 6 5 4 3 2 1

For the love of my life

THE MOUNTAIN

Imagine a mountain . . .
One so familiar you can see it with your eyes closed.
Green in summer, bare in winter, iridescent at sunset,
It's always where it's supposed to be,
right there on the horizon.
You have loved it from afar.

Now imagine deciding to climb that mountain,
Not once but over and over again—
First by the marked path, then by the deer trails,
Then by making your own way up.

One day you pray in the dry streambed.
One day you pray under the stone outcrop.
One day you pray face down in the sweet birch leaves.

My point is, the better you know the mountain—
The more intimate you become—
The harder it is to see it whole,
as something separate from yourself.
You're not looking at the mountain anymore.
You're not even on the mountain.
You're in the mountain's life, as its life pours into you . . .

—Barbara Brown Taylor[1]

[1]Barbara Brown Taylor, excerpt from "Approaching the Mountain in Prayer," in Sarah Bessey, ed., *A Rhythm of Prayer: A Collection of Meditations for Renewal*, 1st ed. (New York: Convergent, 2021), 138–39. Used by permission of the author.

CONTENTS

THE JESUS CLIMB
Journeying from Student to **DISCIPLE**

Dis·ci·ple (di-si´-pehl) n. A student who *continues* on the upward/downward journey of following Jesus, his teachings, and his way of life--the *ascent* of a higher and higher commitment to loving God and neighbor with all their heart, soul, mind, and strength, and the *descent* into a deeper and deeper experience of the intimate, transforming, and other-centered love of God—because they *believe* and have come to *know* him as Teacher, Messiah, Son of God, and Redeemer of the world.

The disciple's *ascent* into a higher and higher commitment to loving God and neighbor with all their heart, soul, mind, and strength.

DESIRE
Follow Jesus as Your Teacher

John 1:36-38 When [John the Baptist] saw Jesus passing by, he said, "Look, the Lamb of God!" When the two *disciples* heard him say this, they followed Jesus. Turning around, Jesus saw them following and asked, "What do you want?"

INSTRUCTION
Reorient Your Life around Jesus's Teachings

John 8:30-32 As he spoke, many believed in him. To the Jews who had believed him, Jesus said, "If you hold to my teaching, you are really my *disciples*. Then you will know the truth, and the truth will set you free."

SURRENDER
Exchange Your Lesser Desires for God's Kingdom

Mark 8:34-35 Whoever wants to be my *disciple* must deny themselves and take up their cross and follow me. For whoever wants to save their life will lose it, but whoever loses their life for me and for the gospel will save it.

COMMUNITY
Make Your Faith Your Own . . . Together!

John 6:66-69 From this time many of his *disciples* turned back and no longer followed him. "You do not want to leave too, do you?" Jesus asked the Twelve. Simon Peter answered him, "Lord, to whom shall we go? You have the words of eternal life. We have come to believe and to know that you are the Holy One of God."

The disciple's descent into a deeper and deeper experience of the intimate, transforming, and other-centered love of God.

I NTIMACY

Pursue the Love and Life of God

John 14:21 Whoever has my commands and keeps them is the one who loves me. The one who loves me will be loved by my Father, and I too will love them and show myself to them.

P RAYER

Bear the Fruit of the Kingdom

John 15:7-8 If you remain in me and my words remain in you, ask whatever you wish, and it will be done for you. This is to my Father's glory, that you bear much fruit, showing yourselves to be my *disciple*s.

L OVE

Give Away Your Life in Other-Centered Service

John 13:34-35 A new command I give you: Love one another. As I have loved you, so you must love one another. By this everyone will know that you are my *disciples*, if you love one another.

E MBODIMENT

Live Everything Jesus Taught—Teach Everything Jesus Lived

Matthew 28:17-21 When they saw [Jesus], they worshiped him; but some doubted. Then Jesus came to them and said, "All authority in heaven and on earth has been given to me. Therefore *go* and *make disciples* of all nations, baptizing them in the name of the Father and of the Son and of the Holy Spirit, and teaching them to obey everything I have commanded you. And surely I am with you always, to the very end of the age.

"We were now able to make out almost exactly where Everest should be;

but the clouds were dark in that direction.

We gazed at them intently through field glasses

as though by some miracle we might pierce the veil.

Presently the miracle happened. . . .

Gradually, very gradually, we saw the great mountain sides and glaciers . . .

until far higher in the sky than imagination had dared suggest

the white summit of Everest appeared."

—George Mallory[1]

FOREWORD

This past summer, I completed my seventh fourteener in Colorado—which refers to hiking to a mountain summit of 14,000-plus feet of altitude. The air is thin, but the payoff is worth it!

I have a passion to get up to the high places of the earth, what climbers and hikers call summit fever! I love the unimpeded, panoramic views, the hypnotic rhythm of my breathing over many hours of exertion, the companionship of fellow adventurers, the euphoric feeling of reaching the heights of creation, and then the satisfaction of descending back to the trailhead.

There are distinct stages in these mountaintop journeys, from the prep and planning to the predawn rising, from staying hydrated and calorie infusions of trail mix to the game-changing shifts that stem from inclement weather. But the climb is always worth it, even when things don't go exactly to plan.

As the ascent begins, the crisp, cold morning envelops you. And there is special delight in passing through dense alpine forests, getting above tree line to the oxygen-deprived regions of tundra, which finally give way at extreme altitudes to snow and ice, rock, boulders, and scree (slippery fields of mini rocks that have been pulverized into gravel by centuries of desolate atmosphere).

Hiking is one of life's highlights for me. What about you? What sparks something like "summit fever"? Where is your journey taking you? What is your destination for your life? Where is your compass pointing?

Whether intentionally or not, each of us wrestles with these kinds of decisions. And how we answer these questions shapes the course, quality, and impact of our lives. *The Jesus Climb*—this wonderful book by my friend Gary Stratton—is a reliable compass and trail guide to the steps ahead of you on the path.

My guess is you have heard of Jesus and probably have warm thoughts about him. Odds are you've made a commitment at some point in your life to follow him. But this book will take you past the paint-by-number depictions of Jesus. *The Jesus Climb* invites you off the paved surfaces of easy answers and formulaic faith. It beckons us to the sheer cliffs of adventure and survival.

The basic orientation of the book is toward understanding Jesus as a rabbi—our master teacher. What can we learn alongside the disciples, both in terms of content and posture? The mountain-climbing metaphor Gary uses ties it all together: moving upward toward God, descending downward in service to others. It is a practical book, too, offering us real tools in our following the trail with Jesus.

I have read hundreds of books on the person and work of Jesus, and *The Jesus Climb* is simply one of the best. First, because the book offers solid dealings with Scripture and terrific personal stories, all supporting a doable program for deeper discipleship. It's a good book, built with sturdy ideas.

Second, the book comes from someone I deeply trust. I've known Gary Stratton for over three decades. He was one of my first professors at university, and I remember being struck then at his personal care for his students, his passion for us to experience God, and his love for Jesus! Since then, his genuine concern for me and his willingness to pray and seek the Lord on my behalf have spoken volumes of the reality of his faith—that he has, in fact, been up the precipitous slopes of being formed like Jesus. Gary is a trustworthy guide to the rare air of true discipleship.

Incidentally, if there is any doubt that ascending with Jesus is worth our time and attention, think of the proof we can see in the attitudes of two famous authors of the Bible: King David and the apostle Paul. After decades of his own searching, the poet-king David writes:

> One thing I ask from the LORD, this only do I seek: that I may dwell in the house of the LORD all the days of my life, to gaze on the beauty of the LORD and to seek him in his temple. (Ps. 27:4)

And the apostle Paul concludes something similar:

> But one thing I do: Forgetting what is behind and straining toward what is ahead, I press on toward the goal to win the prize for which God has called me heavenward in Christ Jesus. (Phil. 3:13–14)

They, too, had a type of summit fever—climbing the holy hill with Jesus!

By the way, this book is already making an impact. As I was reading a digital draft of the manuscript for *The Jesus Climb*, I was sitting next to a woman on a plane. I could tell she had a lot of nervous energy before we took off, and she was busy talking with some friends before switching her phone into airplane mode. We were heading to Dallas/Fort Worth, Texas, from Denver, Colorado (I had just finished my 13.5-mile summit of Pike's Peak). It turned out Amber (my seat mate) was coming from a ghost-hunting trip at the Stanley Hotel, the historic location of Stephen King's film-adapted novel *The Shining*. As we were taking off, she asked me to look at a photo she had taken.

"Does this look like a ghost or a head popping out from behind this fence?"

I stared for a minute or so. "No, it doesn't. Not to me," I said. (It was a grainy photo, and seriously, there was nothing noteworthy to see.)

She seemed genuinely disappointed and asked me to zoom in more. After clarifying that I still didn't see anything weird, I returned to the words on my computer screen. Later, as the plane was landing ninety minutes later, Amber asked what I thought about her, especially since "you are reading about Jesus, and I'm here telling you about ghosts."

I explained, briefly, that I do believe in a supernatural dimension to life, but that I didn't think it was a good idea to hunt for ghosts. "I wonder, though, why looking for ghosts is important to you?"

"Well, my dad died back in May, and I feel so lost. He left me all this money, and I don't know what I am doing. I am just so lost. And I am just looking for a connection—you know, to him, to something!"

It turns out Amber had a Christian background and was experiencing lots of internal conflicts and emotions. I told her about my own profound loss (my late wife passed away from brain cancer). And even as the plane was revving down and we were about to deplane, Amber asked for me to be praying for her.

We all are on a search, aren't we? To restore something that was lost. To find meaning. To fill the deep hurts and traumas we've experienced. To make an impact. To be known.

Amber, like me—and perhaps like you—is on a climb of her own. And this *one thing* I know: *I believe walking with Jesus generates the most freedom and flourishing a person could ever hope to know.* In this way, perhaps like me, this book will help you discover the Real Jesus, not just an Imaginary Jesus.

And that, after all, is worth the climb.

David Kinnaman

CEO, Barna

Author, *Faith for Exiles*, *Good Faith*, *You Lost Me*, and *unChristian*

PREFACE FOR FACULTY
AND CAMPUS LEADERS

This book began as a series of sermons first preached in response to a wave of student awakenings sweeping North America in 1995. At the time, I served as the dean of the chapel at Gordon College in Massachusetts. New England has a long memory. So as the revival spread to our campus, we knew from New England's checkered history in America's first two widespread revivals—the First Great Awakening (1740–42) and the Second Great Awakening (1795–ca. 1835)—that as helpful as an outpouring of the Spirit might be in promoting new or renewed religious commitment in students, revival does not *automatically* produce long-term spiritual growth in individuals nor change unjust structures in society. Without courageous spiritual leadership willing to call for personal and corporate repentance, "times of refreshing . . . from the Lord" (Acts 3:19) could easily lead to the wild enthusiasm and anti-intellectualism of a James Davenport.

We longed for the long-term fruitfulness in church and society achieved by the Second Great Awakening schools, like the intellectual revivalism of school's such as the College of New Jersey at

Princeton under Aaron Burr Sr. and Yale College under Timothy Dwight; the social reform revivalism of abolitionist schools, such as Oberlin College under Charles G. Finney; as well as the visible unity in Christ found in Barton Stone's 20,000-participant multi-denominational communion service at Cane Ridge, Kentucky.[1] In short, we sought to help direct our students from the short-term excitement of day-and-night revival meetings toward the long-term fruitfulness of loving God and neighbor with all their hearts, souls, minds, and strength.

Building on my recent tutelage under Michael J. Wilkins— one of the world's leading scholars on the meaning of "disciple" (*mathetes*) in the New Testament—I worked with newly formed faculty and student leadership chapel committees to reinforce the central theme of Wilkins's scholarship: "Discipleship is not a second step in the Christian life but rather is synonymous with the Christian life."[2] The resulting messages helped guide students toward embracing Jesus's call to follow him from student to disciple by enduring on the "long and costly journey" of growing into a person of transforming love.

The seed of this message grew strong in the good soil of revived hearts. Participation in our voluntary service-learning programs and accountability groups skyrocketed. Increased student engagement in our required chapel services resulted in over 70 percent of our student body saying they "agreed/strongly agreed" with the statement, "Chapel helps me grow in my relationship with God." (We had never broken 50 percent before.) Our voluntary Sunday evening student-led worship service, "Catacombs," outgrew two smaller venues and packed the massive A. J. Gordon Memorial Chapel with Gordon students, as well as college and high school students from throughout the Boston area.

From a faculty perspective, the most encouraging development was the renewal's impact on our academic programs. More than six months after the "revival," both our provost and student body president reported to our president's advisory council that they had never seen classroom morale so high. Not surprisingly, the renewal helped our admissions team secure years of record enrollment. Donors, inspired by what God was doing at Gordon, helped our president and advancement team secure funding for seven new buildings in eight years.

I continued developing these discipleship constructs in Evangelism and Discipleship classes at Gordon; team-taught classes with Mark Cannister and Gary Parrett at Crown College (MN), Bethel University (MN), and Act One: Hollywood; and numerous churches and conferences in between. However, it was not until 2019 that I seriously considered compiling them into a book. One of my Gordon College students, Dr. Kirk McClelland, now a professor of service learning at Johnson University (TN), approached me with an idea. Kirk had recently volunteered to oversee a rebuild of our struggling First-Year Seminar. To my surprise, Kirk insisted, "These students need the message that changed my life at Gordon College. Would you be willing to write a book on discipleship we can use in the class?" I wondered if I could pen a book that both faculty would want to teach and students would want to read, but I was willing to try.

The volume you hold in your hand (or your phone) is my best attempt. Kirk and the faculty and staff in our First-Year Seminar program have helped field test multiple versions. Students have offered significant (and sometimes painful) input. Initial feedback has been good. Aided by a college-readiness curriculum developed by our dean of students, Dr. Andrew Martin Frazier, and spiritual formation retreats made possible by a generous donor, the class exceeded our expectations. Student evaluations collected as part of Dr. Frazier's dissertation research broke all records with an average rating of 4.25 on a 5-point scale.[3]

As what appears to be the first wave of another student renewal sweeps North American campuses, I hope this book will prove helpful to you in guiding your students on their climb toward genuine discipleship—the embodiment of living all that Jesus taught and teaching all that Jesus lived.

Scan the QR code below for faculty and leader resources for teaching The Jesus Climb.

INTRODUCTION

"The most important one . . . is this: 'Hear, O Israel:
The Lord our God, the Lord is one. Love the Lord your God
with all your heart and with all your soul and with all your
mind and with all your strength.' The second is this:
'Love your neighbor as yourself.'
There is no commandment greater than these."

—Jesus of Nazareth (Mark 12:29–31)

You don't always recognize the turning points in your life when they come. I certainly didn't recognize this one. Mrs. Mast called me to her desk during free time and handed me a nondescript hardbound book. Looking me in the eyes, she instructed, "Gary, you might like to read this biography."

Now, Mrs. Mast was not a teacher to be trifled with. She spent her early career serving with the Peace Corps in Africa and now served her public school students with equal fervor. She was the first teacher to ever coax me into living up to some of my academic potential, and she did so with what I can only describe as *tough* love. I spent many a lunchtime longingly looking out her classroom windows at my friends goofing off outside while I sat with Mrs. Mast doing the homework I had neglected the night before.

In other words, I did not want to disappoint her. So rather than ask her what a "biography" was, I gulped, accepted the book with shaking hands, thanked her, then turned and scurried back to my seat to start reading. I read for our entire free period, then the bus ride home, and finished the book by flashlight under my bed covers that night.

I don't recall the name of the book, but I do recall its gist. It was the story of a young man whose family and friends faced a horrifically broken world. Instead of accepting this world like his parents and most of his friends, the hero rose up to make a difference that changed his world for good. Everything within me resonated with his struggle. Maybe every generation believes they are growing up in a dystopian society, but the violence, political graft, corporate greed, and blatant racism that filled the daily news cycle convinced me I faced a similar choice. Something woke up in me that day. I would no longer accept my broken world the way it was. I wanted to help heal it.

I'm certain this was Mrs. Mast's objective. When I returned the book the next day, she didn't commend me for my rapid reading. Instead, she returned the biography to her bookshelf and handed me another. "Do you want to read this one too?" she asked. Like a junkie granted access to a hidden stash, I quickly devoured all fifty volumes in the collection, then discussed them with Mrs. Mast each morning before class.[1] By the end of the year, my desire to make a difference in a broken world was insatiable.

The Question

Fast forward a few decades. Now I am the teacher seeking to cultivate a similar longing in my students. I often begin by asking a question that rarely fails to spark a furious discussion: "Why would anyone want to follow Jesus?"

It's a great place to start a conversation for a group of first-year students who chose to take a class on Jesus. So I usually ask it in our first session together, *the* first college class for many. Then I wait as my students ponder what I am asking.

Let me try to recreate how my students respond in a typical class.[2]

. . . . ༄ . . . .

After a few awkward moments, Caroline said, "I'll share."

"Wonderful!" I replied. (Getting that first student to speak up is always challenging.) "Who is Jesus, and why would someone want to follow him?"

"He's my Savior," Caroline replied. "He died on the cross for me. I follow him to spend my life serving him in return."

"Great answer," I commended her. "But I'll bet there are others who see things differently." I tried to egg them on. "Anyone have a different thought? Who was Jesus, and why would anyone want to follow him?"

"The founder of a colonizing religion," Tony deadpanned as every eye in the room whipped toward him.

"Hey." He held up his hands. "Dr. S. wanted a different answer, and that's what most of my friends think. They think I'm crazy for being a Christian."

"Another great answer," I nodded to Tony. "Thanks for opening things up."

"Well, if we're going to get honest"—Jacob shrugged—"Jesus has never been more than a swear word to me and my friends." Everyone laughed.

"Now we're getting somewhere," I replied. "I appreciate your honesty, Jacob. I'll bet you're not alone on that one." Heads nodded around the room.

"Well, if we're being honest," Alexandra offered, "Jesus Christ meant a lot to my family growing up. My parents would say he's the Son of God who rose from the dead. I thought that way too until high school, but I haven't found a good reason to follow him since."

"I have," Bobby chimed in before I could respond. "I don't want to go to hell. I would dump my belief in Jesus tomorrow and just start doing what I felt like doing if I knew I wouldn't suffer eternal torment for it." Bobby got a lot of head nods as well.

"I don't want to go to hell either," Chris jumped in, "but Jesus promised that if we seek him, we'll get our best life now, here on earth. That's why I'm a Christian." Still more heads nodded.

"Anyone else?" I asked. "Who was Jesus, and why would anyone want to follow him?"

"Well, I grew up in a Muslim family," Steeven spoke up. "We honored Isa—whom you call 'Jesus'—as a messenger of God and a prophet. The Koran even calls him the Messiah. But we hated how Isa's followers treat Muslims, like in the medieval Crusades and the United States today. It seems like people who claim to follow Jesus don't act much like him."

That got even more head nods, followed by a pregnant silence.

Following Jesus

I let that silence rest upon us until Chloe sighed and asked, "Okay, Dr. S., why do *you* follow Jesus?"

"I was hoping you'd ask me that." I smiled as nervous laughter released some of the tension in the room. I continued:

We live in an age full of many and varied opinions concerning what it means to be a follower of Jesus. Attend the right church. Profess the correct doctrine. Vote for the right political party. Shun the wrong friends. Don't use certain words. Abstain from certain drinks. Avoid inappropriate fashions. Boycott certain types of entertainment. It's enough to make your head spin.

In the whirlwind of these conflicting voices, it is easy to miss Jesus's voice telling us what he thought was most important: "'Love the Lord your God with all your heart and with all your soul and with all your mind.' This is the first and greatest commandment.[3] And the second is like it: 'Love your neighbor as yourself'"[4] (Matt. 22:37–39). Or, as the Gospel of John records, "A new command I give you: Love one another. As I have loved you, so you must love one another" (John 13:34).

I follow Jesus because the world is a broken place devoid of such love, and I want to be part of Jesus's mission to put it back together.

My comment got more head scratches than nods. So I added, "Do you all believe the world is pretty screwed up?" This time every head in the room nodded.

I continued, "Jesus came to create a new world where people would truly know God's heart of love and, therefore, love God and one another as Jesus did."

They still looked puzzled, so I added, "Imagine you woke up tomorrow morning and everyone on earth suddenly was as motivated by other-centered love as they are by self-interest today. Maybe some would even be willing to love as sacrificially as Jesus did. How would the world be different?"

"Wars would stop," Ben offered tentatively.

"Exactly!" I encouraged.

"Poverty would disappear," Yenni added.

"Racism would become a thing of the past," Sam insisted.

"Definitely," I replied.

"Mental health would become a priority," Nick suggested.

"Sexual abuse would end," Cara asserted.

"Greed would become unthinkable," Jahson offered.

"Hatred and anger would end," Claire insisted.

"Social media companies would go out of business," Jacob smirked. Everyone laughed.

Finally, Steeven added, "Everyone on the planet would work as hard to ensure no child on earth goes to bed hungry as they do to ensure their own children don't go hungry today."

Everyone was leaning in now as our collective longing for this kind of world filled the room.

The Kingdom

After a few moments of silence, I continued, "Jesus called this new world *the kingdom of God*. It's a kingdom Jesus initiated over two thousand years ago and one day will overcome every force of evil in our world. The kingdom of God becomes a tangible reality wherever God's desires (his 'will') for peace, mercy, righteousness, and justice are done upon the earth as they are in heaven. This kingdom may only be a tiny seed now, but one day it will blossom into a tree whose fruit will feed the world and whose leaves will heal nations. It is the greatest endeavor in human history and the most difficult challenge we'll ever face.

"So, like I said, I follow Jesus because I aspire to become the kind of person who can join him in his mission to set this broken world right, no matter the cost."

After a few moments of stunned silence, Chloe shook her head, looked around the room, and announced, "That sounds amazing! But . . ."

"But what?" I asked when she hesitated.

"But it also sounds TOTALLY IMPOSSIBLE!"

. . . . ⟋ᢙ . . . .

The Jesus Climb

Chloe has a point. It *does* sound impossible. How can broken human beings like you and me ever grow into bearers of God's healing kingdom to a broken world?

After pondering that question for decades, I think I may have found an answer in an unlikely parable. Like most Jewish rabbis of his day, Jesus used parables to reach his hearers' hearts through their imagination.[5] Of course, Jesus crafted his parables from the world of his first-century followers. He told them, "The kingdom of God is like . . ."

a gardner planting a mustard seed (Matt. 13:31–32)

an explorer discovering buried treasure (Matt. 13:44)

a farmer sowing his seed (Mark 4:1–30)

a baker leavening her bread (Matt. 13:33–34)

a king preparing a wedding feast for his son
(Matt. 22:1–14)

His parables "challenged the mind on the highest intellectual level by using simple stories that made common sense out of the complexities of religious faith and human experience."[6] The familiarity of each parable's elements invited his listeners to participate in the story.[7] Then he created teachable moments with surprising twists.[8]

Caught up in the drama, his listeners *experienced* the kingdom of God through their participation in the parable.[9]

I have discovered a parable[10] in our modern world that has helped many of my students begin to imagine how God might heal them and transform them into someone capable of helping heal the world. It is found in the impossible feat attempted by George Mallory and the first explorers who dreamed of scaling the highest point on earth: the summit of Mount Everest. Let's call it the parable of the *Jesus Climb*.

Mallory's Secret

A mountain climber plucked from sea level and suddenly dropped on the 29,035 foot[11] summit of Mount Everest would immediately collapse into a coma and die within hours. The atmosphere in Everest's *death zone* (above 26,250 feet) contains less than one-third of the oxygen available on an ocean cruise, not nearly enough to sustain human consciousness, let alone life.

Despite this seemingly insurmountable obstacle, the day came when humans stood atop Everest. This miracle was made possible by an accident of history. As George Mallory and other climbers in the first British expedition explored Everest's terrain, they quickly realized the task would be more like a giant construction project than a race.[12] So they established a *base camp* in the relatively thick atmosphere of 17,500 feet, then developed a series of *expedition camps*—each approximately 1,500 feet higher than the last—stretching toward the summit.[13] Mallory sought only to stockpile each expedition camp with the cumbersome supplies needed for their final assault on the summit. He didn't realize that his strategy served an even greater purpose—transformation!

As team members moved painstakingly back and forth between the base camp and higher and higher expedition camps, they gradually acclimatized to thinner and thinner air on each

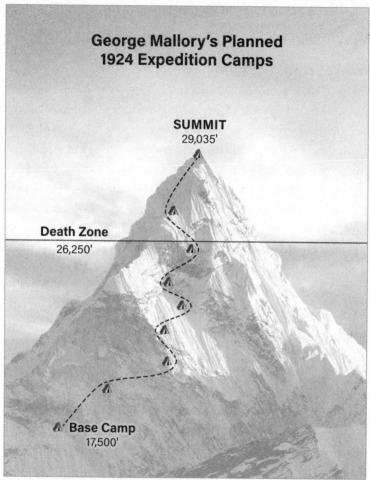

**George Mallory's Planned
1924 Expedition Camps**

SUMMIT
29,035'

Death Zone
26,250'

Base Camp
17,500'

Figure 0.1. Mallory's Upward/Downward Journey [Locations are approximated to fit a single viewpoint]

ascent, then recovered their strength during each descent back to base camp. Slowly, this upward/downward journey altered their entire physiology. Their red blood cell count doubled. Their bodies drew up to ten times more oxygen per breath.

Soon, Mallory's climbers could ascend to heights that would have been impossible for them to survive just a few months earlier. Their upward/downward journey transformed them into people who could climb in Everest's death zone long enough to reach the summit.

Jesus's Secret

I hope I'm not pushing the metaphor too far in exploring how Jesus guided his first followers along a climbing trail similar to Mallory's acclimatization process. Jesus knew that any follower plucked from their first spiritual steps and suddenly forced to stand atop his 29,035-foot call to love God and neighbor wouldn't fare any better than a mountain climber dropped on top of Everest. Loving God with everything within us and loving others—even our enemies—as much as we love ourselves are not heights climbed easily nor quickly. By the time followers reach the zenith of spiritual altitude, the self-interest that drives our everyday life grows much too thin to love God above all else, let alone love others more than we love ourselves. Jesus knew his followers would never survive life in this spiritual death zone long enough to reach the summit of transforming love.

Despite this seemingly insurmountable obstacle, the day came when Jesus's first followers—flawed and broken people very much like you and me—reached the spiritual summit of other-centered love. By focusing on Jesus's teaching on what it meant to be his *disciple*—a word used over 260 times in the New Testament—rather than on the word *Christian*, a word used only three times, it is possible to discern how Jesus accomplished this miracle. Using an acclimatization strategy not unlike Mallory's, Jesus set up a *base camp* in the relatively thick spiritual air of his followers' first spiritual steps. Then, by his teaching and example, he guided his followers along a series of *expedition camps* leading toward the summit along two interrelated yet distinct pathways. First, we have the *ascent* of a higher and higher commitment to loving God and neighbor with all our heart, soul, mind, and strength via the camps

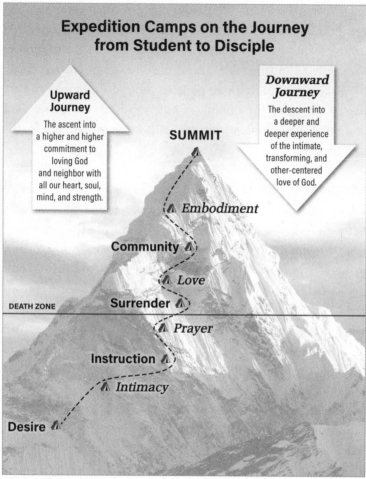

Expedition Camps on the Journey from Student to Disciple

Upward Journey
The ascent into a higher and higher commitment to loving God and neighbor with all our heart, soul, mind, and strength.

Downward Journey
The descent into a deeper and deeper experience of the intimate, transforming, and other-centered love of God.

SUMMIT

Embodiment

Community

Love

DEATH ZONE

Surrender

Prayer

Instruction

Intimacy

Desire

Figure 0.2. Jesus's Upward/Downward Journey

of **Desire, Instruction, Surrender,** and **Community.** Second, we find the *descent* into a deeper and deeper experience of God's intimate, transforming, other-centered love through the expedition camps of **Intimacy, Prayer, Love,** and **Embodiment.** (Yes, the eight camps form the acrostic DISCIPLE. What can I say? I'm a teacher.)

In the process of this upward/downward journey, the very nature of Jesus's disciples underwent a profound transformation.

Their spiritual red blood cell count doubled. Their every spiritual breath drew ten times as much grace. Slowly, they acclimatized to find themselves completely different people on the summit of their Jesus Climb than they were at the base camp of his initial call to "Follow me." Since then, no Jesus follower in human history has ever reached the summit of Jesus's radical call to love God and others without following the pathway he marked out for his first students.

Landmarks Not Standards

I designed this book to help you better understand what it meant to follow Jesus as a disciple in his world so you can better navigate what it might mean for you to follow Jesus in your world today. I bring very little mountain-climbing experience to the task. Still, decades of helping my students learn to follow the course marked out by Jesus for his students has taught me much about what it takes to become a spiritual mountain climber today.

I will also include stories from the biographies of some of history's greatest spiritual climbers. Their journeys convince me that it is possible to follow Jesus into a life so awash in the breathtaking intimacy of the love of God that climbing the heights of other-centered love for God and others becomes possible. And, lest you despair of ever reaching such heights, I will also include a few stories from my own stumbling efforts to follow Jesus up the mountain. (Scan the QR codes at the end of each chapter for even more personal stories available online.)

As we explore the principles and processes in the following chapters, please don't fall into the trap of viewing these "expedition camps" as standards to earn God's approval or avoid his wrath. I intend them to serve only as a map for your upward/downward journey following Jesus. I do not claim that this upward/downward framework is the only way to look at following Jesus, or even the best. Yet I have found that looking at Jesus through this lens opens the possibility of seeing him in an entirely new light. Just as we can often see the light of a star more clearly by looking at it with our peripheral vision, exploring the Jesus Climb can help us see aspects of following him not visible from other vantage points.

As Chloe so aptly proclaimed, transformation into the kind of person who can join Jesus in his mission to heal a broken world may seem *totally impossible*. But it's not. It simply requires a determination to continue following Jesus up the mountain of faith, no matter the cost—a journey that begins at the base camp of **Desire**.

Scan the QR code below for the backstory on Gary's early discipleship climb.

PART ONE

ASCENT

The disciple's *ascent* into a higher and
higher commitment to loving God and neighbor
with all their heart, soul, mind, and strength.

ONE

DESIRE

Sequencing Jesus

"The next day John was there again with two of his disciples.
When he saw Jesus passing by, he said,
'Look, the Lamb of God!' When the two disciples
heard him say this, they followed Jesus.
Turning around, Jesus saw them following and asked,
'What do you want?'"

—John 1:35–38

In 1875, three French scientists launched their hot-air balloon into the morning sky, hoping to soar to a world record for human altitude. The trip started well, but when their balloon finally returned to earth, two scientists had died, and the third lay unconscious and deaf for life. The balloon's altimeter recorded they reached no higher than twenty-eight thousand feet—one thousand feet *lower* than the newly crowned "highest mountain on earth." Not surprisingly, most educated men and women concluded that the French balloon experiment had proven once and for all that Everest could never be climbed.

George Mallory was not among them. The descendant of a long line of ministers, Mallory's contagious optimism fueled his life. As one climbing mate exclaimed, "I never saw anyone show such ecstatic delight as George in the presence of the mountains."[1] Mallory first fell in love with climbing when a professor invited him on a trip to the Alps. Upon returning to campus, Mallory honed his climbing technique scaling the brickwork and chimneys of college buildings as crowds of classmates gathered to cheer him on. Upon graduation, Mallory shaped his teaching career around mountain climbing in the Alps and rock climbing in Wales, quickly earning a reputation as one of the greatest climbers in the world. When the British Alpine Club and Royal Geographical Society joined forces to outfit three expeditions to Everest (1921–24), George was the logical choice to lead the climbing team.

When Mallory hit the international speaking circuit to fundraise for their expeditions, a *New York Times* reporter asked him, "Why do you want to climb Mt. Everest?" Mallory's famous reply, "Because it's there," tells us as much about the kind of men and women who seek such adventure as any other statement in climbing history. While most mortals regard the dangers of altitude sickness, avalanches, storms, and frostbite as sufficient reasons to remain at sea level, Mallory viewed such challenges as mere stepping stones on his grand quest.

Before the 1924 expedition, he wrote: "One must conquer, achieve, get to the top; one must know the end to be convinced that one can win the end—to know there's no dream that mustn't be dared."[2] Mountain climbers call this passion *summit fever*. As climber Jon Krakauer explains, "There are many fine reasons not to go. But summiting Everest is an intrinsically irrational act. A triumph of **Desire** over sensibility."[3]

The same could be said for the first students to follow Jesus.

The College of Jesus

Imagine you are dashing around your room tomorrow morning in one last frantic attempt to find a matching pair of socks when you're startled by an unexpected knock. Moaning, you throw open your door. Then you stare in disbelief. Standing before you is Jesus and a small band of disciples. Without saying hi, Jesus looks deep into your eyes and speaks just two simple words: "Follow me."

Then, without waiting for your response, he arches his eyebrow, cocks his head, and slowly walks back down the hall.

What would you do?

A) Laugh hysterically and look for hidden cameras.
B) Slam the door in his face and return to looking for your socks.
C) Fall on your knees in worship.
D) Pump your fist and follow him down the hall while texting your mom, "I got in!!!"

As strange as it may sound, if this encounter happened to you during the earthly life of Jesus, your most likely response would have been (D) Pump your fist and follow him down the hall while texting your mom, "I got in!!!" (Probably followed by many celebratory emoji.)

Why? Because long before Jesus founded a church, he first established a "college," and getting into such a college was a big deal.

Let me explain.

Jewish Higher Education

We often project our contemporary understanding of Jesus onto a man who, at least at the beginning of his public career, fit a relatively normal role in his society. No one viewed him as the Son of God or a prophet. They saw him as a teacher, also known as a rabbi.[4]

His students called him Teacher.[5] The crowds addressed him as Teacher.[6] Even his enemies referred to him as Teacher.[7] The role of teacher explains everything from his selecting disciples to travel with him to the place of honor he was afforded in synagogues. And as a teacher, Jesus followed most of the standard educational practices of his society.

In Jesus's day, Jewish boys entered what we would call an "elementary school" around the age of seven, with the goal of mastering the first five books of the Jewish Scriptures—the Torah.[8] Around age thirteen, the most promising students advanced to the Jewish version of secondary school in a "study house" led by their village rabbi. Their "high school" curriculum included the study of the Prophets (like Isaiah and Daniel), Writings (such as Psalms and Proverbs), as well as the Talmud—the collected sayings of history's greatest rabbis. And if you think today's Advanced Placement courses are demanding, by the end of high school, Jewish secondary students were often expected to memorize the entire Torah.

Then, and only then, could the most remarkable high school students gain acceptance into the Jewish version of "college"— studying with a great rabbi. Becoming a disciple of any rabbi in Jesus's day meant apprenticing in your rabbi's teachings and way of life in the same way you might apprentice to learn a trade. The curriculum comprised two primary texts: (1) the scroll of the Torah, and (2) the life of your rabbi, who was considered "Torah transformed into an embodied form of human being."[9] In Jerusalem and other wealthy communities, this meant studying in a house of learning connected with the temple or a major synagogue. For everyone else, this meant studying with a traveling rabbi, also known as a "sage."[10]

Rather than leaving home to move into a dorm room or take online classes from home, Jewish college students became permanent commuters. They followed their rabbi night and day as he traveled from village to village, teaching in various synagogues and study houses. This living and learning process occurred in almost every possible venue—on the road, over meals, and in the marketplace.[11] Good students stuck so closely to their teacher that by the end of the day, they found themselves covered with the dust kicked up by their master's feet. A saying written down after Jesus's day could have been circulating during his ministry: "Let your home be a meetinghouse for the sages, and cover yourself with the dust of their feet, and drink in their words thirstily."[12]

Through it all, students strove to attain the prerequisite mastery of the Scriptures and Talmud necessary to become rabbis themselves. Most dreamed of one day establishing a "college" of their own. As another later rabbinic saying codified, "He who has students who in turn have students of their own is called 'Rabbi.'"[13]

Burning in the Snow

All this is to say that studying with a traveling rabbi involved a selective admissions process through which a mere handful of the best and brightest students strove for admission into a few elite "colleges." The story of the student who grew into one of Judaism's most famous and influential rabbis illustrates this point. Hillel longed to know the Word of God with such great intensity that he moved his family from Babylon to Jerusalem so he could study with the greatest Torah scholars in the world.[14] What Hillel didn't realize was that rabbis of such stature didn't allow just anyone into their college. They accepted only those students whose village rabbi could vouch for their hunger for God's Word. Fifteen hundred miles from home, Hillel lacked the appropriate connections or letter of recommendation. His application was rejected.

Undaunted, Hillel worked as a woodcutter to provide for his family. Eventually, he earned enough money to bribe the guard at the gate of the rabbinic school, allowing Hillel to enter the grounds. Once inside, he would climb onto the roof of the study house and listen to the great rabbis teach until late into the evening.

One night, the weather grew unusually cold. Soon snow began to fall. Hillel was so enthralled with the rabbis' words he refused to leave his illicit perch. Slowly, hypothermia began to lull him into a sleep from which he might never recover. Fortunately for Hillel, heavy snowfall in Jerusalem was an unusual event. The rabbis wanted their students to marvel upon the beauty of the city of peace blanketed in a symbol of God's mercy. So, despite the cold, they threw open their classroom windows. It wasn't long before someone spotted Hillel's near-frozen body.

The rabbis directed students to climb onto the roof and rescue the unconscious Hillel, whom they revived with warm soup and a hot bath. The rescue revived his academic career as well. The rabbis were so impressed with the depth of Hillel's hunger for God's Word they immediately granted him admission to their college.

Hillel went on to become the greatest Torah scholar of his generation and an important figure in early Christianity. It is likely that Hillel and/or his disciples were among the scholars who examined another famous young man known for his hunger for God's Word—the twelve-year-old Jesus (Luke 2:46–48). Later, one of Hillel's best students, Gamaliel, defended Jesus's followers when they were dragged before the Jewish court of law (Acts 5:33–40). Gamaliel, in turn, taught yet another zealous student who came to Jerusalem to study God's Word—Saul of Tarsus, who would later become known as the apostle Paul (Acts 22:3).

While Hillel's snow story was likely embellished over time (the final version had him covered in more than four feet of snow), it illustrates the nature of higher education in Jesus's day. On the one hand, discipleship was common in the first-century world. Greek philosophers had disciples. Jewish rabbis had disciples. John the Baptist had disciples. Even the Pharisees had disciples.

On the other hand, admission to such a learning community was a rare and precious attainment. We're accustomed to more than half of American high school graduates attending college. In first-century Israel, only a handful of young men got such an opportunity. Like Hillel in the snow, each student had to convince their rabbi they possessed the ability and the **Desire** to devote their lives to learning and applying their teacher's sayings and way of life.

Transfer Students

Rabbi Jesus was no different. The first "prospective students" to visit his college weren't your classic freshmen. According to the Gospel of John, they were transfer students from the college of John the Baptist. John's teaching ministry attracted enormous crowds who flocked into the wilderness to listen and be baptized. His central message, "Repent, for the kingdom of heaven has come near" (Matt. 3:2), created tremendous anticipation for the coming of God's Messiah. Remember, Israel was a Roman-occupied nation. They longed for deliverance. And they yearned for God's promised Messiah to lead them. Now John seemed to be promising them just what they wanted.

Messiah means "anointed one" and pointed to how God "anointed" leaders with his Spirit when he called them to serve as prophets and kings in the Old Testament. While the crowds sought a king to crush the Romans and free God's people politically, John the Baptist proclaimed a prophet anointed with God's Spirit to liberate Israel spiritually. No matter which type of Messiah someone wanted, John's ministry was a big deal in Israel—national news. Social media couldn't get enough of him. Jewish people everywhere waited in breathless anticipation for John the Baptist to reveal the identity of God's Messiah.

Behold the Lamb

We don't know how long this went on. Some scholars believe John's public career lasted only a few months. Others think he may have preached for over a decade. What we do know for certain is that his ministry lasted long enough for John to choose disciples for his own rabbinic college.[15] The Baptist taught his students how to pray (Luke 11:1) and fast (Matt. 9:14) as they waited for the coming of God's Messiah (Luke 7:19).

Then one day, it happened. Jesus appeared at the Jordan River, asking John to baptize him. At first, John refused, citing his unworthiness. Jesus insisted. Then when John relented and baptized Jesus, the promised anointing of the Spirit of God fell upon Jesus in such a tangible way John perceived it fluttering out of heaven like a dove. Suddenly, a voice from the heavens called out, "You are my Son, whom I love; with you I am well pleased" (Mark 1:11).

Pretty heady stuff.

Yet here's the strange thing. Instead of calling for a press conference like you'd expect, John the Baptist reserved his big reveal for a much more private audience—two of the students in his college.[16] Andrew and John the Beloved[17] "just happened" to be with John the Baptist when Jesus walked by. The Baptist suddenly let two of his favorite students in on the secret all of Israel was longing to hear: "Behold! Here, at last, is the Lamb of God!" (Mic drop!)

Admissions Visit

Andrew and John the Beloved were no idiots. They saw the moment for what it was—John the Baptist's nomination of his best students to be examined by the great rabbi. It was their opportunity for an "admissions visit" to the greatest college the world has ever known on the first day it opened! Without missing a beat, Andrew and John the Beloved fell into step behind Jesus. Jesus likely knew exactly what was going on. John the Baptist was his cousin, equipped from birth to prepare the way for Jesus's ministry. They may even have discussed this process: "John, you scour the country looking for the best and brightest spiritual students and then send them to me."

Andrew and John the Beloved's admissions interview began with Jesus's first question. He turned to them and asked, "What do you want?" (John 1:38).

It sounds like an innocuous question. Yet it is laced with double meaning. On the one hand, it sounds like a bit of a brush-off, like, "Why are you following me, stalkers?" But a more literal translation of the phrase would be, "What are you seeking?" Jesus was asking these potential students if they were Hillels. Were they willing to do anything—even freeze to death—to become his students, or were they just looking for an "easy A" and a diploma?

Andrew and John the Beloved seem to know exactly how to play this admissions game. In their culture, it would be rude (and possibly humiliating) to directly ask a rabbi for an entrance examination. So, they asked indirectly, "Rabbi, where are you staying?" This, too, is full of double meanings. On the surface, it is an indirect way of saying, "Could we hang out with you?" But in the code words of rabbinical college admissions, it also means, "Can we become your students?"

To his wannabe disciples' delight, Jesus responded, "Come and you will see," which is yet another delightful double meaning, signifying both "Let's hang out" and "Come and learn." And learn they do. Jesus's version of college is so interpersonally intensive that he spends the entire day with them. We don't know what they discussed, but Andrew and John the Beloved must have done well enough on their entrance exam. John the Beloved's Gospel tells us how they were allowed to accompany Jesus as he traveled to Cana, Samaria, and Jerusalem (John 1–4).

Later,[18] Jesus found them while they were going about their normal life, washing their nets after a frustrating day in their family's fishing business. That's when Jesus finally called them into full-time rabbinic training, saying, "Come, follow me . . . and I will send you out to fish for people" (Mark 1:17). He even provided them with the financial aid of a miraculous catch of fish to feed their families while they were gone (Luke 5:1–11). Is it any surprise that they immediately left their nets and followed him? Other rabbis may have rejected such a ragtag bunch of fishermen, tax collectors, and zealots, but Jesus had found the kind of students he was looking for. Like Hillels in the snow, their **Desire** to learn from Rabbi Jesus eclipsed their every other desire.

What Do You Want?

Should following Jesus be different today? Some might say, "Of course it should. After all, the purpose of following Jesus today is to get your ticket to heaven. All you need to do is accept Jesus into your heart, and you're good to go, right?" But why wouldn't Jesus ask his potential followers today the same question he asked Andrew and John the Beloved: "What do you want?"

Don't miss the simplicity of this question, nor its depth. Typically, when we ask someone "What do you want?" we're referring to their feelings, tastes, or opinions—something like, "What do you feel like right now? A burger or chicken?" But Jesus is asking about more fundamental desires that go far deeper—more like, "What are you searching for?" or "What are you directing your life toward?" Our constantly changing emotions and opinions lack any real staying power. Our **Desires** are more focused and enduring. They reveal the "inclination of the will"—the underlying motivational disposition of our heart.[19]

FEELINGS	DESIRES
Superficial	Deep
Fleeting	Long-lasting
Often inconsistent with our values and beliefs	Consistent with our values and beliefs
Often overwhelm our entire being: heart, soul, mind, and strength	Normally flow from our entire being: heart, soul, mind, and strength
Cannot be controlled, only responded to, nor are they morally "good" or "bad"	Can be directed toward ends that are good or bad, healthy or unhealthy
Result in unintentional actions, behaviors, and habits	Result in intentional actions, behaviors, and habits

Figure 1.1. Feelings versus Desires

For instance, the soccer team may not *feel* like exercising this afternoon, but their **Desire** to win their next game will help them overcome that feeling. The choir may not feel like rehearsing this evening, but their **Desire** to perform with excellence at their next concert will overcome these more transitory emotions. A student may not feel like giving up her weekend to write a research paper, but her **Desire** to get into a top graduate school will cause her to order her life *against* her mere preferences.

Now suppose that student completed her paper with a note to her professor saying, "I just want you to know that I am taking your class because I want to become a medical researcher and find a cure for the brain cancer that took my sister's life. I am willing to do anything, even extra reading or additional assignments, to master this subject. Don't go easy on me."

How might that professor respond? (After they faint.) Most likely, she will invite the student to her office for deeper conversations and into her laboratory for personal mentoring. Why? Because that's the kind of learner every professor dreams of finding.

Professor Jesus is no different. He sought students with the character qualities educator Angela Duckworth described in her book *Grit*. Students who possess both "passion and perseverance." Students who are marked by a "ferocious determination that plays out in two ways." First, students who are unusually resilient and hardworking. Second, students who know "in a very, very deep way what it [is] they want."[20] In other words, he is looking for disciples who **Desire** him as their Teacher.

Sequencing Jesus

This might sound obvious, but it is not. Many "Christians" today **Desire** only the benefits of following Jesus—God's blessing on their life or a free ticket to heaven—but they do not organize their life around Jesus's calling to be his students. They call themselves Christians yet make no effort to master his teachings or follow his commands. They peer at the summit of loving God and neighbor with everything within them and declare, "No, thank you!" They are like modern adventure tourists who visit Everest's base camp merely to take in the view. They don their impressive Christian climbing gear, sing countless Christian songs about Jesus's sacrifice and love, but never intend to follow him up the mountain.

My trigonometry teacher, Ms. Elliot, helped me see how devasting such an approach can be. One day, she caught me completely off guard by asking, "Did you ever move between school districts as a child?"

Now, you need to know that I entered her trigonometry class as a certifiable math failure. Not only had I just flunked her first unit test, but I also scored so low on the math section of my SAT that there was no way I could ever get in to any of my first-choice colleges.

I knew it. My parents knew it. Even my friends knew it.

Ms. Elliot had other plans.

First, she invited me to come to her classroom during lunch. Then, instead of teaching me trigonometry, she asked me if I moved as a kid!

I tentatively answered, "Twice." Then added quickly, "Why does that matter?"

She arched her brow, placed a blank piece of paper on the table, and asked, "Have you ever heard of the educational principle known as *sequencing*?"

"No," I replied warily.

Stifling a smile, she calmly explained, "Sequencing means a student's potential for new learning depends on their existing knowledge base. Facts build upon facts. Concepts build upon concepts."

Then she drew the following chart on the blank piece of paper.

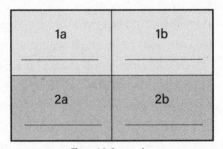

Figure 1.2. Sequencing

She asked me, "Suppose I wanted to get from box 1a to box 2b on this chart. How could I get there?"

It seemed rather obvious, so I said, "Well, you would have to go through either box 1b or 2a?"

"Exactly!" She beamed. Then she wrote words in the boxes.

1a Arithmetic	1b Algebra
2a Geometry	2b Trigonometry

Figure 1.3. Math Sequencing

I saw her point right away.

"No one can go straight from arithmetic to trigonometry. You have to build algebra or geometry into your knowledge base first," she explained.

I nodded as she continued, "Of course, the easiest learning pathway builds upon *both* algebra and geometry before you try to tackle trig. That gives your brain two learning routes, known as *cue associations*, to build upon."

That made sense to me, but I still didn't know how it would help me get in to a good college.

Then she asked, "How old were you when you moved?"

My eyes filled with tears (very much against my will) as I tried desperately *not* to feel the connection she was making.

She rubbed my arm and consoled me, "Did you feel hopelessly lost in your math classes?"

"Both times," I croaked.

Then she made me look her in the eye as she spoke the words that changed my academic life, "Gary, you are not bad at math. You simply have holes in your math sequencing. There are parts of your knowledge base that are missing. Your brain doesn't have enough cue associations to figure out the problems I gave you."

Suddenly she had my full attention.

"It will take a lot of hard work," she offered, "but if we can figure out what went wrong with your sequencing, we can plug those holes so trigonometry will make sense to you. Are you willing to give it a try?"

I was. For the next six months, I spent countless lunch hours in Ms. Elliot's classroom filling in the holes in my math sequencing. My understanding of math grew exponentially. My trigonometry grades slowly improved. The ultimate test of my progress—retaking the SAT—came six months later. To my amazement, I scored *one hundred and ten points* higher in math.

Ms. Elliot cried. My mom cried. Even some of my friends cried. And I got into all my first-choice colleges. (Otherwise, you probably wouldn't be reading this book.)

Sequencing Discipleship
In addition to saving my academic career, Ms. Elliot also helped me understand why so few professing Christians today become world changers. You see, if you ask most American Christians, "Who is Jesus?" their answer often goes something like this: "Jesus is the Son of God who came to earth to be my Savior." Now there is nothing "wrong" with this response. The problem is that it is incomplete; it skips right over the foundational concepts of Jesus's ministry. On a Ms. Elliot sequencing chart, it might look something like Figure 1.4 below.

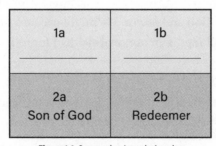

Figure 1.4. Sequencing Jesus in America

For the first disciples, following Jesus did not begin with following Jesus as the Son of God or Redeemer. He started their understanding of his identity at a much more foundational level. While each of the four Gospels has its own distinct emphasis,[21] their general sequence on a Ms. Elliot chart looks something like Figure 1.5 below.

1a Teacher	1b Messiah
2a Son of God	2b Redeemer

Figure 1.5. Sequencing Jesus in the Gospels

Following Jesus in the Gospel Sequence

In other words, following Jesus as Teacher and Messiah is *foundational* to following Jesus as Son of God and Redeemer. Without that foundation, the typical American "Son of God who became my Savior" understanding of Jesus is bound to be as problematic for following Jesus as my defective math sequence. We're trying to solve trigonometry-level spiritual problems with holes in our arithmetic- and algebra-level foundational understanding of Jesus. If we don't first learn to follow Jesus as our Teacher (and Messiah), we probably aren't going to be able to accurately solve for following him as Son of God and Savior. We might even decide that following Jesus's teachings is an optional element for following Jesus.

Base Camp

This makes the **Desire** to follow Jesus as your Teacher the *base camp* of all true discipleship. No matter what other *expedition* *camps* we climb to, no matter how high the altitude or how thin the air, the **Desire** to follow Jesus as our Teacher is the foundation to which every disciple must return again and again. Such **Desire** was the starting point for every disciple of every rabbi in Jesus's day—be they Hillel in the snow or James and John the Beloved on the road with Jesus. Dare we make commitment to Jesus something less today?

I believe the first key to seeing more Jesus followers transformed into world healers is to admit that the Bible teaches us that the first step toward genuine faith is a **Desire** to follow Jesus as our Teacher. Not a one-time decision to escape hell but a ferocious determination to follow him up the mountain that we must return to again and again. Flowers move their faces to follow the path of the sun because the sun is their one true **Desire**. Jesus is looking for students who long for him in the same way: men and women who long to climb to the summit of genuine discipleship "because *he* is there."

A Climbing Guide for the Disciple's Ascent into
DESIRE

Cultivating a **Desire** to follow Jesus as your Teacher can be challenging, especially if you grew up in a faith community that underemphasized this foundational element of discipleship or in no faith community at all. Here are a couple of training practices that have helped me.

Assess and Refocus Your Discipleship Sequence
Assessing Your Jesus Sequence: Start analyzing your Jesus "sequencing" using my hack of Ms. Elliot's chart in Figure 1.6 on the next page.

1a Teacher _____ %	1b Messiah _____ %
2a Son of God _____ %	2b Redeemer _____ %

Other?

_____   _____ %

_____   _____ %

_____   _____ %

Total (all boxes)   100%

Figure 1.6. Your Jesus Sequence

1. Fill in the blanks in Figure 1.6 with how often you think of Jesus in each aspect of his identity mentioned: Teacher, Messiah, Son of God, Redeemer, Savior, Swear Word, etc.
2. Now, reflect on any gaps in your sequencing of Jesus's identity. For instance, how has your sequencing influenced your relationship with him? Do you see any "holes" in your sequencing? How do those holes affect your **Desire** for him to teach you?

Refocus your Jesus Sequence: If you wish to refocus your view of Jesus, try one of the following approaches.

If you are already a Jesus follower but now realize there's a hole in your sequencing of his identity, just tell him you want to be his student and ask him to teach you. Then, seek to learn and follow his teachings and way of life more intentionally. I would also suggest you occasionally pray to him as your "Teacher." You may be amazed how addressing him as his first students did can help you reboot your relationship with him.

If you're *not* currently a Jesus follower or have *never* sought to follow him, just tell him you want to be his student and ask him to teach you. Then, seek to learn and follow his teachings. Don't try to figure out what hoops you must jump through or rush to "accept" Jesus as one of his upper box identities. That's not how he started with his first students. Start by following him as your Teacher.

A student once asked one of my mentors, "Why is Jesus such a big deal? And, if he is a big deal, how would you advise me to experience him?"

His response surprised me and the student: "Don't start by trying to believe the big truths about Jesus. Start by putting into practice the things he said, trusting him to be right about it. And if you do that, you will gradually find out what a big deal he is."

This is exactly what happened to me (scan the QR code at the end of the chapter to learn more), and it is some of the best advice I could give anyone just starting out on their Jesus Climb.

Jesus's first students were baptized (literally "immersed" or "purified") in water as an outward symbol of their inner **Desire** to learn to follow everything he taught (Matt. 28:19–20). Today, many find baptism (or *confirmation*, or *re-baptism* for those baptized by their parents in their childhood) a profoundly meaningful initiation rite into a life of following Jesus.

Whether you are already following Jesus or want to start, you may be unsure as to what to say to him. If so, pray something like this: "My Teacher, I **Desire** to be your student. I want your teachings to guide my life. Help me become the kind of person who can love God and others with everything within me so I can join you in your mission to heal a broken world."

Invite Jesus to be Your Teacher in Every Area of Your Life

Another practice that greatly influenced my **Desire** to follow Jesus as my Teacher was inviting him to be my Teacher in *every* area of my life.

For instance, shortly after I started following Jesus, my secular school literature instructor, Ms. Steffney, assigned a comparison paper between two of George Bernard Shaw's plays: *The Devil's Disciple* and *Pygmalion*. I finished reading the plays and took pages of notes. Yet, after an entire weekend of trying to find a theme for comparison, I could not come up with a single promising idea for my paper. Part of the problem was George Bernard Shaw's faith, or lack thereof. He held Christianity in such low esteem that it leaked all over his plays. Giving up, I put my head down on the desk and said to no one in particular, "This is impossible."

I immediately sensed my Teacher say, "I was waiting for you to say that."

His words were so real I bolted upright and said aloud, "You can teach me about George Bernard Shaw?"

I didn't get an answer. Yet as I thought about it, the idea made sense. I mean, who knew Shaw's plays better than Jesus? So, I prayed something like, "Jesus, I want to follow you as my Teacher, so please teach me not about the Bible but about these plays." Then I added, "And just so I know I'm actually learning from you, could you somehow help me write something that uses George Bernard Shaw's skepticism to glorify you?"

Well, Jesus didn't send an AI angel to write my paper for me, but as I prayerfully looked over my notes for the umpteenth time, I discovered a theme spanning both plays that had previously illuded me: *hypocrisy*. George Bernard Shaw hated hypocrites even more than he hated Christians, making them the butt of his jokes in both plays. So, I charted an outline and started writing.

Three hours later, I finished the five-page paper. I didn't know if it was good or not, but it did seem to glorify God. I still remember the final line: "But woe to those two-faced Aristocrats and false Christians who honor God with their lips when their hearts are far from him, for they shall be cast beneath the pen of George Bernard Shaw where there will be much weeping and gnashing of teeth."

I turned it in before the deadline (barely) and even told some of my friends about my "divine paper encounter." (They all feared for my sanity.) But when Ms. Steffney returned our work a few days later, she not only gave me an A, she also distributed a copy of *my* paper to everyone in the class as an example of writing with excellence. She even read my last paragraph aloud, declaring it, "more than a mere last-minute inspiration." Of course, she took my name off it, but my friends knew who wrote it and laughed and laughed.

My **Desire** to follow him as my Teacher increased exponentially and changed how I approached my entire life, from sports to relationships to academics. I wasn't a world-healer yet, but now I knew I had a brilliant teacher whose expertise extended far beyond merely religious activities. And so do you!

I would highly recommend you ask him to be your teacher in every area of your life. When we do, we're ready to climb for the next expedition camp on the *Ascent* toward the summit of genuine discipleship: **Instruction.**

*Scan the QR code below for the backstory on Gary's climb toward **Desire**.*

TWO

INSTRUCTION

The Unexpected Kingdom

"If you hold to my teaching, you are really my disciples.
Then you will know the truth, and the truth will set you free."

—Jesus of Nazareth (John 8:31–32)

Even experienced mountain climbers often fail to grasp the true challenge of summiting Mount Everest. Towering five and a half miles above sea level—the cruising altitude of commercial jets—Everest is nearly unique among the world's mountains. Only three Asian countries—Nepal, Pakistan, and China—contain peaks higher than 26,250 feet (the beginning of the human "death zone"). Outside of Asia, just a few dozen peaks (mainly in the Andes range of South America) stand even as tall as Everest's base camp of 17,500 feet! This means that unless a climber has summited a peak in the Himalayas or the Andes, Everest's 29,035-foot zenith is over 12,000 feet *higher* than any mountain they have ever climbed.

This lack of a comparative reference point often lulls even seasoned climbers into a false sense of complacency during the first stage of their journey. Jon Krakauer writes of his first attempt to climb Everest: "The first six days of the trek went by in an ambrosial blur. The trails took us past . . . thundering waterfalls, enchanting boulder gardens, burbling streams. . . . Unburdened and unhurried, caught up in the simple joy of walking in an exotic country, I fell into a kind of [euphoric] trance."[1]

It isn't hard to imagine how Jesus's first students might have felt the same way during the first stage of their discipleship journey. Assuming that the Gospel of John uniquely describes the earliest phase of Jesus's ministry,[2] the true challenge of following Jesus probably wasn't immediately evident to his first followers. The thundering waterfall of Jesus driving the money changers from the temple (John 2:13–22), the enchanting boulder gardens of his conversations with both a privileged rabbi (3:1–21) and a shunned Samaritan woman (4:1–42), and the burbling stream of their teacher changing water into wine at a wedding celebration (2:1–11) could easily have contributed to Jesus's students falling into a kind of euphoric trance.

They had found God's Messiah! Surely Jesus was about to take up arms and vindicate Israel against their pagan occupiers, "winning the theological battle by military force."[3] As they juggled their day jobs with trips to travel and study with Jesus, they must have felt like they had front-row seats to the apocalypse. Think of it! Jesus was grooming them for leadership positions in his coming kingdom. It was everything they could ever desire and more.

Higher than Imagination Dared to Suggest

Or was it? On June 12, 1921, George Mallory climbed a hill hoping to gain his first glimpse of Everest. Mists and thick clouds occluded the view, but the ever-determined Mallory checked his map and riveted his attention on the spot where he believed Everest stood. He wrote: "Gradually, very gradually, we saw the great mountainsides and glaciers, until far higher in the sky than imagination had dared suggest, the white summit of Everest appeared."[4]

I wonder if Jesus's first students felt the same way the day they caught their first glimpse of the true cost of discipleship—the day King Herod threw John the Baptist into prison. Matthew tells us, "When Jesus heard that John had been put in prison, he withdrew to Galilee. . . . proclaiming the good news of the kingdom" (Matt. 4:12, 23).

As a reader, you can sense the sudden change in intensity. So could Jesus's disciples. First, their rabbi canceled his national travel itinerary, moved to Capernaum, and limited his movements almost exclusively to the Jewish backwater of Galilee. Then Jesus revoked his students' part-time studies and called them to begin traveling with him full-time. Finally, Jesus launched a series of one-person TED Talk conferences designed to reinforce and expand on the exact same message as the now-imprisoned John the Baptist had taught. "The time has come. . . . The kingdom of God has come near. Repent and believe the good news!" (Mark 1:15).

Jesus's students quickly realized their rabbi's curriculum might differ slightly from what they expected. Beginning with the Sermon on the Mount (Matt. 5–7) and continuing through a vast array of public (and private) teaching sessions,[5] Jesus's authoritative teaching and extraordinary healing ministry began to draw enormous crowds. Having summarized his message as repentance in view of the coming kingdom, Jesus now began to explain exactly how someone who wanted to be ready for God's kingdom should live.

Still clinging to their hope for a place of privilege in God's coming reign, Jesus's students slowly began to realize that repentance was not a one-time event but a process of reorienting their lives to the worldview of their teacher. Gazing up at Jesus's towering vision of the kingdom of God, they must have begun to wonder if their powers of imagination were sufficient for the task.

A Vision of the Kingdom

American Christians often define the kingdom of God as "the *place* we are going to live with God when we die." For the Jews in Jesus's day, the kingdom of God was "the *time* when God is coming to live with his people on earth." Rabbis had been scouring the Old Testament prophecies for centuries, searching for when and where the kingdom of God would appear. They knew that the promised kingdom of heaven was, in Scot McKnight's words, "God's Dream Society on earth, spreading out from the land of Israel to encompass the whole world."[6] While Jesus's vision of the kingdom of God never contradicted this prophetic idea, his students never could have imagined how God's kingdom was coming into the world.

Jesus knew his students were trapped in flawed biblical interpretations and cultural understandings of the kingdom of God. So he used his Galilean teaching tour to launch an assault on his students' limited imaginations, utilizing a dizzying pedagogy of metaphors, illustrations, parables, discussions, sayings, and miracles. Walter Brueggemann refers to this kind of ministry as *prophetic imagination*. It is designed "to nurture, nourish, and evoke a consciousness and perception alternative to the consciousness and perception of the dominant culture around us."[7]

To his students' surprise, Jesus's Galilean vision of the kingdom of God omitted any mention of a military or political revolution. Instead, Jesus spoke of a spiritual revolution beginning in the human heart. Only those who sought after God with purity of heart would see him. God's upside-down kingdom was coming for those who worked for peace, not war; those who were merciful, not vengeful; and those who hungered for righteousness, not exaltation. The kingdom of God belonged to the poor over the rich, the meek over the powerful, the young over the mature, and the persecuted over their oppressors.

Jesus cast a vision for a world in which everything taught by Moses and the prophets was not only fulfilled but exceeded. The righteousness of the kingdom would extend past mere outward conformity to the Law, "You have heard it said . . . ," and transform the motives and intentions of the heart, "But I say unto you . . ." Instead of merely legislating against murder, adultery, divorce, and revenge, Jesus preached a revolution of the heart capable of eliminating anger, hatred, cursing, lust, dishonesty, and oppression as well. Religion would no longer be a tool for impressing your tribe with your piety or judging everyone outside your tribe with damnation. Prayer, fasting, and even giving to the poor would be done in secret for no greater reason than the good of others and the pleasure of a heavenly Father who longs to pour out the blessings of heaven.

Leadership in Jesus's kingdom would be distinguished by self-sacrificing love and service, not self-centered power and the domination of others. So don't "network," trying to maneuver your way up the social ladder by throwing parties for people who can hook you up. Throw parties for those who can never pay you back: the poor and the outcasts, the widows and orphans, the tax collectors and sinners.

Astonishingly, Jesus's vision extended even to Israel's greatest enemy: the Romans. God's kingdom of transforming love would eventually cover them as well. So don't work for their violent overthrow; pray for them! Turn the other cheek. Go the extra mile. Don't resist evil with evil. Overcome evil with good. Be perfectly merciful, seeking to bless both evil people as well as the good, just as your heavenly Father does.

The triumph of the kingdom of heaven won't come like an invading army. It will start as small as a mustard seed—but look out. Over time it will grow and spread like a mustard plant until it covers the entire garden. Slowly the leaven of God's kingdom of love will fill the whole earth.

No wonder his students' imaginations were insufficient for the task. As they listened to his teaching day after day, Jesus left them with only two choices:

1. Drop out of Jesus's college, or
2. Repent!

Repentance

The word the Gospel writers use for "repent" (*metanoeo*) probably doesn't mean what you think it does. It signifies "to think after," and by extension, "to think differently," "change your mind," "reconsider your thinking," or simply "rethink your thinking." *Metanoeo* is nearly identical to what educators today refer to as *metacognition*. Metacognition describes our unique human ability to "think about our thinking." For instance, students who fail their first college exam because they waited to study until the night before their test employ metacognition when they rethink their life and devise a better strategy for preparing for their next exam.

This means that when Jesus called people to "Repent for the kingdom of God is near,"[8] he wasn't saying, "Turn or Burn!" or whatever else a street preacher might say today. He wasn't even telling them to give up their personal sins and pray a prayer of faith. He was **Instructing** Israel, "Rethink your life in light of the reality of how God is now breaking into the world." As N. T. Wright explains, Jesus was communicating: "Give up your agendas and trust me for mine."[9]

Continuing in the Word

Of course, reorienting your life to Jesus's kingdom vision doesn't happen all at once. Matthew's and Mark's summaries of Jesus's Galilean ministry, "Repent for the kingdom of God has come near," are precisely that: *summaries* of everything he taught about the kingdom and how to "repent" in light of it. Two essential collections of Jesus's teachings—commonly called the Sermon on the Mount (Matt. 5–7) and the Sermon on the Plain (Luke 6:20–49)[10]—each conclude with the parable of the wise and foolish builders. The story draws a sharp distinction between those who hear Jesus's teachings but don't put them into practice (the foolish) and those who dig deep to base their lives upon them (the wise). Jesus isn't talking about following a few sentimental platitudes. He wants students willing to dig deep enough to make his wisdom the rock-solid foundation of their lives. Only then can they withstand the inevitable storms of life.

So how is this foundation built? The Gospel of John describes an instance when Jesus experienced what you and I might consider a real breakthrough in his teaching. He had been teaching about spiritual freedom during the Jewish festival celebrating Israel's sojourn in the wilderness after they experienced freedom from slavery in Egypt. He appears to have succeeded. John the Beloved tells us, "Even as he spoke, many believed in him" (John 8:30).

I suspect a typical minister today would chalk this up as a win, take an offering, and go home. Not Jesus. He wanted to evoke more than a one-time decision. He wanted to build a lifelong foundation. So, he responds to the Jews who had believed him, "If you hold to my teaching, you are really my disciples. Then you will know the truth, and the truth will set you free" (John 8:31–32).

The Greek word for "hold to" or "continue" refers not only to a length of time but also to a depth of experience. It is often translated as "abide" or "dwell." When you abide in your home, you

71

don't just stay in your house for a long time (unless you're in a pandemic lockdown). You live there. That means when you continue in Jesus's teachings, you don't just keep reading them (though that is a good start), you live in them and allow them to live in you.

This fits perfectly with the general practices of Jewish higher education. Today, we tend to think of college as the transmission of information. The most successful students are those who can regurgitate the most facts on a test. However, Jewish education sought the impartation of life. The process began with the mastery of content—the Torah and your rabbi's interpretations of the Torah—but the goal was to write the Torah on the pages of your heart, enlightening the soul and transforming the life.

This process came to be known as "meditation." For instance, God instructs Joshua, "Keep this Book of the Law [the Torah] always on your lips; meditate on it day and night, so that you may be careful to do everything written in it. Then you will be prosperous and successful" (Josh. 1:8). The book of Psalms begins with God's promise that those who meditate day and night on the Torah become as fruitful and drought-proof as trees "planted by streams of water . . . whatever they do prospers" (Ps. 1:1–3). Moses instructed Israel that the key to loving God with all their heart, soul, and strength was day-and-night meditation on the Torah. Meditating on God's Word was the key to becoming the kind of person who could follow God's law and build the foundation of a flourishing society and personal life.

Jesus expected his students—those who were "truly his disciples"—to evidence a similar commitment to *his* teaching. A true student—a true disciple—doesn't merely *start* following Jesus. They *continue* mastering and following Jesus's teaching. It is the only way his students could know the truth, repent of their flawed thinking about the kingdom, and know the freedom of living out kingdom righteousness. This means repentance is not a one-time event but an ongoing process—continuing in Jesus's teaching until it transforms your thinking and way of life.

Is such a transformation possible? The life of Daniel Alexander Payne indicates that it is.

Called to Educate

"I have set you apart to educate yourself so you can be an educator of your people!"

Daniel Alexander Payne (1811–93) was stunned. All he asked from God was wisdom for his future. Now he "heard" a voice calling him to devote his life to instruction so he could instruct others. How could this voice be God?

Payne had only recently begun following Jesus when God answered his Sunday school teacher's prayer for revival. But God calling an orphaned eighteen-year-old "free person of color" to educate his people at a time when slaves nearly outnumbered Whites seemed crazy. Yet as Daniel continued in prayer, he became more and more certain that these impressions were "divine and irresistible."[11] Daniel Alexander Payne obeyed.

Reorienting His Life

Payne began to devote every free moment of his life to study. He taught himself to read not only the English Bible but also Greek and Hebrew. With few schools open to Black students, Payne found tutors to teach him Latin, literature, history, mathematics, and science. He used every penny he earned as a carpenter's apprentice to purchase books. He studied till midnight each night, slept until four a.m., then read by candlelight until he opened the carpenter's shop at six the following morning.

After years of rigorous preparation, Payne felt ready for the second phase of God's call—to become an educator. Just before his twentieth birthday, he used his status as a freeborn Black man to don the customary teaching robes of his day and open his first school. His students were other free Black boys and girls and slaves whose masters wanted them educated. It proved a wise financial strategy in a city where slaves nearly outnumbered Whites.

Despite early financial sacrifices and accusations of practicing sorcery for the way he integrated the work of the Spirit into his teaching, Payne slowly grew his school to sixty students. His rigorous and inspirational teaching left people "amazed at the quality of the students and the curriculum."[12] Daniel rejoiced that he had been obedient to Jesus's voice and found his life's work, but he could never have imagined how much more Jesus had in mind.

Kingdom Heartbreak

In 1835, a series of revolts led by educated Black slaves resulted in the South Carolina legislature banning the teaching of slaves. Forced to close his school, Payne began to doubt his calling and his God. He wrote in his journal, "If God does exist, is he just? If so, why does he suffer one race to oppress and enslave another, to rob them by unrighteous enactments of rights, which they hold most dear and sacred?"[13]

After many days of lament, Daniel sensed the Spirit assuring him: "With God one day is as a thousand years and a thousand years as one day. Trust in me, and I will bring slavery and all its outrages to an end." Suddenly, Daniel knew his call to education was about more than just his own future. It was about God's kingdom breaking into the sinful world and setting things right for his people.

Kingdom Trailblazer

That night, Payne woke with a vivid dream in which he fled to the north wearing his teaching robe. When he shared the dream with a Lutheran minister who had been tutoring him in the sciences, the pastor not only helped him find the money to sail to New York City but also provided Payne with a letter of recommendation to a friend who pastored there. The New York minister provided Payne with food and lodging and put him in touch with Lutheran church leaders looking for a "talented, pious young man of color devoted to the intellectual, moral, and social elevation of free colored people." Ten days after landing in New York, Payne had a full-ride scholarship to study at the Lutheran seminary in Gettysburg, Pennsylvania.

Payne studied theology and obtained permission to use an empty seminary building to establish a school for local Black children. This second school brought him into contact with leaders of the nation's first Black denomination—the African Methodist Episcopal Church (AME). Payne spent the remaining fifty years of his life training clergy and other leaders in the AME, who elected him as their sixth bishop in 1852.

The summit of Daniel's journey of **Instruction** came in 1863 as a teacher and member of the board of trustees of Wilberforce University in Ohio. Founded by White Christians to educate Black students, the university's finances depended on tuitions paid by Southern plantation owners seeking to educate their mixed-race sons born from the sexual abuse of their slaves. When the Civil War stopped the flow of these students north, the university trustees voted to close the now-bankrupt school.

This was the moment Jesus prepared Daniel's imagination to seize. Even though he had only twenty dollars in his pocket, Daniel prayed quickly and then boldly motioned: "Trusting in God, I buy the property of Wilberforce for the African Methodist Episcopal Church."[14]

It was a daring and brilliant act of faith. Wilberforce became the nation's first Black-led university. It helped launch a movement that started more than one hundred historically Black colleges and universities (HBCUs), training many Black leaders and guiding countless students to a deep faith rooted in the life of the mind, the life of the Spirit, and the teachings of Jesus. As Payne wrote in his report to the Ohio Department of Education shortly before his death:

> Every year the school has been visited with a gracious revival of religion, and many of the pupils have been made the happy subjects of a work of grace which is deemed all-important to their usefulness in life. This benevolent scheme is based on the supposition that the colored man must, for the most part, be the educator and elevator of his own race in this and other lands. Hence, a leading object of the Institution is to educate and thoroughly train many of them for professional teachers, or for any other position or pursuit in life to which God, in His providence, or by his Spirit, may call them.[15]

Award-winning historian James T. Campbell concludes, "No single individual . . . did more to shape the trajectory and tone of African Methodism."[16] By following Jesus's call of **Instruction** even when his imagination was insufficient for the task, Daniel Alexander Payne became the kind of person who could change his world for good.

A Climbing Guide for the Disciple's Ascent into
INSTRUCTION

I can't say my journey of **Instruction** has been nearly as dramatic as that of Daniel Alexander Payne's, but I can say several practices have helped me on my climb toward this crucial expedition camp.

Journaling

The first practice that helped me on the journey toward **Instruction** was keeping a logbook, or a journal. A few months after I began to follow Jesus as my Teacher, I grabbed an empty spiral notebook and wrote:

> The purpose of this logbook is
>
> 1. to remind me of all Jesus teaches me so I don't forget so easily;
> 2. to record all the difficulties Jesus has pulled me through so I don't lose heart;
> 3. to help me better understand myself so I know how I react to different situations and temptations;
> 4. to help me grow closer to God by disciplining myself to spend more time with him daily and assessing how connected I've been to him each day.

Since that day, I've filled an entire bookcase with journals. Making journaling a regular habit has dramatically helped me listen to his **Instruction** more intentionally and apply it in my life more diligently.

Mary of Bethany's Prayer

A second practice grows from the example of a disciple who exemplified a commitment to Jesus's **Instruction**: Mary of Bethany. The Gospel of Luke relates the pivotal moment in her relationship with her Teacher.

> As Jesus and his disciples were on their way, he came to a village where a woman named Martha opened her home to him. She had a sister called Mary, who sat at the Lord's feet listening to what he said. But Martha was

distracted by all the preparations that had to be made. She came to him and asked, "Lord, don't you care that my sister has left me to do the work by myself? Tell her to help me!"

"Martha, Martha," the Lord answered, "you are worried and upset about many things, but few things are needed—or indeed only one. Mary has chosen what is better, and it will not be taken away from her." (Luke 10:38–42)

Mary recognized the incredible opportunity Jesus's visit presented to her. In any other setting, Mary would have had to follow the social customs of her day and sit in the back row of Jesus's "classroom." Not today. Sitting in her own home, she had the right to sit close to her family's guest of honor. As Jesus took the rabbi's chair in her living room, no one could stop Mary from pushing her way forward to sit at Jesus's feet, soaking in every word he spoke.

"Mary's Prayer" simply turns Mary of Bethany's example into a prayerful posture.

Step One: Grab a Bible, and find a quiet place to sit. Then pray, "Jesus, my Teacher, help me follow Mary's example. Help me push away the distractions of everything else that needs to be done to spend these moments sitting at your feet, listening carefully to your teaching."

Step Two: Open your New Testament to one of Jesus's teaching sessions. (The Sermon on the Mount in Matthew chapters 5 to 7 is a great place to start.) Listen for your Teacher's voice to direct you to a particular saying or verse as you read. Then silently meditate on that teaching.

Step Three: Once your attention fastens onto a particular teaching, keep "chewing" on Jesus's words over and over as you pray, "Teacher, help me listen to what you taught us so I might better follow this teaching in my life today." You may be amazed by the things you can now see in the text when you start looking at it from the perspective of sitting at his feet as his devoted student.

Step Four: Continue to sit at the feet of Jesus all day by repeating the saying over and over while you put on your makeup, shave, drive, stand in line, etc. One of my mentors, Klaus Issler, uses sticky notes to create "pause" buttons and sticks them all over his home, his car, and his office to remind himself to stop, look, and listen to Jesus and his teachings.[17] By following Jesus as your teacher throughout your day, you may begin to notice his teachings begin to flow from your Bible into your *life*.

Anxiety

Sound a little vague? Allow me to describe one area of my life where I immediately began to see the value of following Jesus's **Instruction:** *anxiety*.

I grew up in a family culture of continual critique. It helped me develop world-class expertise in what psychologists call "automatic negative thoughts" (ANTs for short). Like the bone-chilling Dementors of the fictional world of Harry Potter, the kiss of an ANT sucked all happiness and hope from my heart and the ability to think from my mind. No matter what challenge I faced, I simply *knew* I was going to fail. Why? Because my Dementors kept flooding my mind with "helpful" declarations such as "You are such a loser. You are going to fail. Why do you even try?" In baseball, a Dementor's kiss could transform me into a trembling little leaguer. In test taking, I "froze up" even when, moments before, I knew all the answers. And don't even let me get started on my legendary problems sinking basketball free throws.

What's worse, ANTs all too easily become generalized. That's when our anxiety goes from fearing what is happening to us *now* to catastrophizing about what *might* happen in the future. Suddenly, my thoughts would bounce between infinite possible negative scenarios. Every academic test, athletic contest, or social situation became a new occasion to listen to the voices of my Dementors and crumble.

Fortunately for me, Jesus often addressed this very human experience in his teaching. One day as I sat "at Jesus's feet" reading through his Word, I was struck by this passage in the Sermon on the Mount:

> Do not worry about your life, what you will eat or drink; or about your body, what you will wear. Is not life more than food, and the body more than clothes? Look at the birds of the air; they do not sow or reap or store away in barns, and yet your heavenly Father feeds them. Are you not much more valuable than they? (Matt. 6:25–26)

I found the words profoundly reassuring in the moment. But I knew that just reading them once wasn't enough to make any real difference in my life. Automatic negative thoughts are precisely that: automatic![18] My lifelong mental habits and decision-making patterns proved much more stubborn than a bit of light Bible reading. No matter how hard I tried, I could not get my brain to give up its ANTs. That's when I first discovered the power of "Mary's Prayer." By spending significant time—sometimes an hour a day—prayerfully meditating upon Jesus's teachings on God's loving care for us, they began to soak into my everyday life.

Whenever I felt the paralyzing grip of anxiety, I would pause, turn aside, close my eyes, and imagine myself sitting at Jesus's feet "listening to what he said." As I began to mediate on the teachings I had been soaking in, I could then "repent"—rethink my thinking—and begin to reprogram my anxious thoughts. By meditating on Jesus's prophetic imagination of God's love, I could often (not always) withstand a powerful anxiety storm beating on my life.

I wish I could say this process was as instantaneous as quoting a Bible verse or calling out "Expecto Patronum."[19] It would take years of meditation, prayer, healthy relationships, and professional counseling to truly alter the anxiety-driven default mode of my soul. Still, even in those early years, the practice of meditating on Jesus's teachings throughout the day began to loosen the grip of my Dementors and significantly decrease my anxiety in test-taking, athletic competitions, and social situations.[20] (Even if I never did become much of a free throw shooter.) Life became a much less foreboding place as I spent consistent time striving to "sit at Jesus's feet" like Mary of Bethany. Only then was I was prepared to *follow* Jesus's **Instruction** in the heat of my daily battle against anxiety. As I began to reorient my life around Jesus's teaching, I slowly began to *know* the truth. And slowly, the truth began to set me free.

All this led me to the next expedition camp on the Jesus Climb: **Surrender**.

*Scan the QR code below for the backstory on Gary's climb toward **Instruction**.*

THREE

SURRENDER

"Whoever wants to be my disciple must deny themselves and take up their cross and follow me. For whoever wants to save their life will lose it, but whoever [surrenders] their life for me and for the gospel [of the kingdom] will save it."

—Jesus of Nazareth (Mark 8:34–35)

Walking on a flat surface in the oxygen-rich atmosphere of sea level, a moderately fit adult takes approximately one complete breath for every eight steps they travel.

> INHALE—step, step, step, step
> EXHALE—step, step, step, step

Climbing a flight of stairs, that same adult might only be able to take four steps per breath.

> INHALE—step, step
> EXHALE—step, step

At Everest's base camp (17,500 feet), even trained climbers consider themselves fortunate if they manage one step per breath.

> INHALE, EXHALE—step
> INHALE, EXHALE—step

When alpinists climb above base camp, the ratio inverts. Progress is now measured not in steps per breath but in *breaths per step*.

> STEP—inhale, exhale, inhale, exhale
> STEP—inhale, exhale, inhale, exhale

As Everest climber John Krakauer explains: "The higher I got, the more laggardly I moved. I slid my jumar clip up the fixed line with a gloved hand, rested my weight on the device to draw two burning, labored breaths; then I moved my left foot up and stamped the crampon into the ice, desperately sucked in another two lungfuls of air; planted my right foot next to my left, inhaled and exhaled from the bottom of my chest, inhaled and exhaled again; and slid the jumar up the rope one more time. . . . In this agonizing fashion I climbed . . . , progressing in increments calibrated in inches."[1]

When a climber enters Everest's famous *death zone* (above 26,250 feet), every cell in their body begins to die from lack of oxygen. No one can remain in the death zone for more than a few hours, so above 26,250 feet, their climb literally becomes a race against death. In this extremely low-oxygen atmosphere, most mountaineers require *four* gasps per step.

> STEP—gasp, gasp, gasp, gasp
> STEP—gasp, gasp, gasp, gasp

When climbers reach the notorious forty-foot cliff known as "Hillary Step," less than two hundred vertical feet from the summit, climbers without supplemental oxygen tanks discover that their journey is now measured not in breaths per step but *steps per fall*! Super climber Reinhold Messner describes the final meters of his Everest journey this way: "I was in continual agony . . . I can scarcely go on. I consist only of will. After each few meters this too fizzles out in unending tiredness. Then I think nothing. I let myself fall, just lie there. For an indefinite time, I remain completely irresolute. Then I rise to make a few steps again."[2]

In the death zone, falling is not necessarily failing. It is part of the journey. Falling becomes failure only if the climber fails to get up. This, then, is the secret to summiting Everest:

> STEP—gasp, gasp, gasp, gasp
> FALL—gasp, gasp, gasp, gasp
> RISE—gasp, gasp, gasp, gasp
> STEP—gasp, gasp, gasp, gasp
> [REPEAT]

Upon This Rock

Is following Jesus into the "spiritual death zone" of genuine discipleship any different? If the spiritual journey of Simon Peter—the valedictorian of Jesus's college—is any indication, then Everest's death zone and discipleship's death zone have much in common. Simon Peter's career in Jesus's college was one of firsts. He was one of the first four students Jesus blessed with a miraculous catch of fish. He was one of the first two students Jesus called to follow him on his Galilean journeys. He was the first student Jesus chose as an apostle. Most importantly, he was Jesus's first student to pass Jesus's ultimate essay question, "Who do you say that I am?"

It was a watershed moment in Peter's spiritual journey. Gradually and by increments calibrated in inches, Peter had climbed to a mind-numbing spiritual height as the first student to finally declare:

> STEP—gasp, gasp
> "You are the Messiah . . ."
> STEP—gasp, gasp
> ". . . the Son of the living God!"

While it is doubtful Peter grasped the profound theology implicit in his words, he had somehow ascended to a spiritual height far above any student in history. He now recognized that Jesus was not only his rabbinic Teacher and Israel's Messiah but also the Son of the God of Israel.

Simon Peter earns the first "A+" ever granted in Jesus's "Who am I?" curriculum. Jesus not only commends him, but he also promises he will be the first of many:

Blessed are you, Simon son of Jonah, for this was not revealed to you by flesh and blood, but by my Father in heaven.[3] And I tell you that you are Peter, and on this rock I will build my church, and the gates of Hades will not overcome it. (Matt. 16:17–18)

Pretty heady stuff. Peter must have assumed he had just aced his final exam and could now take his well-earned position at Jesus's right hand while the Messiah vanquished Rome and set up the kingdom of God on Earth.

Into the Death Zone

But a funny thing happened on the way to Peter's plan for a management career in Jesus's monarchy. "Who am I?" was not Jesus's *final* exam essay question. It was his *midterm*. Instead of vaulting Peter and his classmates directly into prime leadership roles, Jesus immediately led them into the spiritual death zone. Matthew's Gospel tells us:

> From that time on Jesus began to explain to his disciples that he must go to Jerusalem and suffer many things at the hands of the elders, the chief priests and the teachers of the law, and that he must be killed and on the third day be raised to life. (Matt. 16:21)

This was not the career path Peter had in mind. Jesus's star pupil immediately objected in no uncertain terms. Taking his Teacher aside (the same Teacher he just identified as "the Son of the living God" a minute ago), Peter rebuked Jesus! "Never, Lord! . . . This shall never happen to you!"

Now remember, Peter was deeply committed to the pathway of following a great rabbi. He possessed a deep and burning **Desire** to follow Jesus as his Teacher by mastering Jesus's **Instruction**. But Peter's **Desire** to follow Jesus depended upon Jesus coming through for him on why he started following him in the first place. Peter was willing to follow the Messiah into victory. Now Jesus began to **Instruct** him to give up his lesser **Desires** and follow his teacher into death.

Jesus turned to Peter and said, "Get behind me, Satan! You are a stumbling block to me; you do not have in mind the concerns [**Desires**] of God, but merely human concerns" (Matt. 16:23). In one interaction, the same student who discovered the bedrock foundation for the church's future becomes the mouthpiece of Satan himself.

gasp, gasp, gasp, gasp—FALL!

To make matters worse, before Peter can even catch his breath, Jesus begins teaching his students that the Messiah isn't the only one heading for suffering. He tells them, "*Whoever* wants to be my disciple must deny themselves and take up their cross and follow me. For whoever wants to save their life will lose it, but whoever loses their life for me and for the gospel will save it" (Mark 8:34–35—italics mine).

It isn't hard to imagine how disorienting these words must have been for Jesus's students. For them, a cross wasn't a piece of jewelry to wear around their neck or a decoration on a sanctuary wall. A cross was an instrument of torture and death. The only reason anyone ever picked up a cross was to carry it to their own execution. How could God's Messiah be killed, and why would Jesus want his students to be willing to die a torturous death as well?

Surrender and Genuine Repentance

To say Peter is gasping for breath in a low oxygen environment is a gross understatement. He is in the death zone—the third essential camp for any student in the college of Jesus seeking to become a genuine disciple: **Surrender**.

Over the following weeks, Jesus's new upper-division course in **Surrender** begins to fill more and more class hours in his climbing college. And for the rest of Peter's spiritual journey, the story will remain essentially the same.

In the rarefied air of **Surrender**, every step is marked not only by labored breathing but often by a fall as well.

> Peter is the only student to walk on water with Jesus. STEP—gasp, gasp

> Peter is the only student who needs to be rescued from the wind and waves when his faith fails him. FALL—gasp, gasp

Peter is one of only three students allowed to witness Jesus's glory on the Mount of Transfiguration. STEP—gasp, gasp

Peter is the only student who suggests that a building program is the best response to glory—one tent each for Jesus, Moses, and Elijah. FALL—gasp, gasp

Peter is the only student who promises to follow Jesus to his death. STEP—gasp, gasp

Less than twenty-four hours later, he is the only student who denies he knows Jesus rather than face arrest! And he does it *three times*!

Gasp, gasp, gasp, gasp—**FALL!!!**

Like climbers who collapse atop Hillary's Step just a few yards from Everest's summit, Peter lies sprawled on the mountainside, unable to rise. Surely this is where his spiritual journey finally ends.

Yet Jesus knows something no one on earth would ever suspect, something even Peter himself could never imagine—Peter has fallen, but his faith has not failed!

You read that right.

Peter's faith had not failed.

On the night before he committed his act of triple-betrayal, Jesus looked deep into Peter's eyes and told him: "Simon, Simon, Satan has asked to sift all of you as wheat. But I have prayed for you, Simon, that your faith may not fail. And when you have turned back, strengthen your brothers" (Luke 22:31–32).

What? Jesus knew Peter would be sifted. Jesus knew Peter would fall. Yet Jesus also knew Peter was going to turn back. Even in this horrific failure, Peter's journey of repentance is about to scale higher heights than he could have ever imagined possible. These trials have not ruined Peter's faith. They have refined his faith and proven it genuine, the same imagery Peter uses near the end of his life. Reassuring his own students who are facing seasons of testing, he writes:

> Now for a little while you have had to suffer grief in all kinds of trials. But remember, to determine if a piece of ore actually contains gold, a smelter must place it into a fiery furnace. The same thing happens when you go through trials. True faith—of greater worth than gold—comes out of the furnace of our trials not only proven genuine but also purified of impurities. (1 Pet. 1:6–7 GDS)

This is Jesus's goal for the graduates of his college: *genuine faith*. He allows their ascent of discipleship to push them not only to their limit but *beyond* their limits to help them obtain it. Why? Because just like a climber on Everest, a disciple's fall does not necessarily mean failure. Falling becomes failing for one reason alone—if we fail to get up and continue our climb.

Because genuine repentance grows only from **Surrender**, the difference between the true disciple and the false disciple is this: the true disciple keeps getting up, keeps seeking, keeps repenting, keeps straining upward. The false disciple does not.

The Great Exchange

Surrender is essential to our faith. Remember, the first expedition camp for following Jesus is **Desire**. At the earliest stages of following, all that matters is that you are moving toward Jesus, wanting to be with him, to abide (remain) in his presence. This is the beauty of Jesus's ministry: he accepts everyone! Children, lepers, gentiles,

Samaritans, Roman centurions, tax collectors, and even "sinners" are welcome. The kingdom of God is a *centered set* rather than a *bounded set*.[4] Jesus is not interested in excluding people. All that matters is that someone keeps moving toward him. The prostitute who seeks first the kingdom of heaven is closer to God than the religious leader who perfectly keeps the letter of the law. Jesus knew exactly *why* each person followed him and seemed to have little problem with any of the reasons people started their journey.

However, Jesus also knew that the very **Desires** that first motivated someone to start following him are the most likely to get in the way of continuing their spiritual journey. For instance, if you start following Jesus only because you want to defeat the Romans, and Jesus **Instructs** you that the kingdom of God is about turning the other cheek, your faith in him as Messiah is genuine only to the degree you **Surrender** your desire by "repenting" (turning from) your agenda to Jesus's.

This often happens today. Some churches tell people, "Come to Jesus, and your **Desire** for wealth or blessings will be fulfilled." Who wouldn't want to follow a Messiah who wants to make you rich? But what happens when you don't get what you want out of Jesus? Do you stop following? Many do. Why? Because they have only been following Jesus "as a means to an end" to get what they **Desire**, not to follow his **Desire** (will/kingdom) expressed in his **Instruction**.

But as Peter saw so clearly, Jesus is not merely a great rabbinic teacher. He is the Son of the living God. All other allegiances must bow before the King of the kingdom of God. He came into the world to lay down his life to make a new world of God's loving kingdom possible. If you genuinely **Desire** his **Instruction**, your journey will eventually bring you into the death zone, where you will need to **Surrender** everything, as Jesus did. This is why the *ascent* of genuine discipleship progresses through both seasons of growth and seasons of sifting when we must count the cost of exchanging the lesser **Desires** of our life for an unquenchable thirst for the kingdom of God.

For instance, the Gospel of Luke tells us Jesus turned to a large crowd traveling with him and said: "If anyone comes to me and does not hate father and mother, wife and children, brothers and sisters—yes, even their own life—such a person cannot be my disciple" (Luke 14:26). Now, Jesus was not telling his students to text their parents, "I'm learning a lot about following Jesus at college. So, I just want to let you know, I HATE YOU!" No, he is simply pointing out the relationships that are most likely to rival allegiance to him. He knew if your **Desire** for your family and friends is stronger than your **Desire** for him, you will eventually choose your family and friends over him. It's that simple.

He didn't mean you can't love your family and friends, only that you can't use them as an excuse for not obeying his call. In fact, in another setting, Jesus clarifies, "Anyone who loves their father or mother *more* than me is not worthy of me; anyone who loves their son or daughter more than me is not worthy of me" (Matt. 10:37—italics mine). The operative word here is "more."

Family of origin was the most important relationship in the ancient world—much like the nuclear family we build with our significant others today. Jesus knew family was the relationship most likely to compete with allegiance to the kingdom. Remember, his highest student learning outcome was educating students capable of loving God with all their heart, soul, mind, and strength. If that's your educational goal, you can't allow any other "god" to come between you and the one true God.

The Call of Love

The Gospel accounts of the wannabe disciple known as the "rich young ruler" help illustrate how Jesus's call to **Surrender** is rooted in divine love. The rich young ruler desperately wanted entrance into the kingdom of God and diligently worked to keep all the commandments of the Old Testament law to accomplish this. Jesus didn't condemn him for his zeal. Instead, he personalized his call to **Surrender** to the young man's unique situation: "One thing you lack. . . . Go, sell everything you have and give to the poor, and you will have treasure in heaven. Then come, follow me" (Mark 10:21).

Mark's Gospel tells us that at this, "the man's face fell. He went away sad, because he had great wealth." He **Desired** the kingdom of God, but not at the cost of **Surrendering** his **Desire** for riches (and the sense of identity and privilege they afforded him). Rather than following Jesus's **Instruction**, he walked away downhearted.

But here's an essential factor Mark wants us to notice. Jesus's words to this "rich young ruler" are an act of *love*. Mark tells us that before Jesus issued his **Instruction**, "Jesus looked at him and *loved* him" (Mark 10:21—italics mine). Mark wants us to know God is not a monster in the sky seeking to take away the things we love. Divine love wants the very best for us, to help "save" and "find" our true life in the things that cause us to come fully alive (Mark 8:35). Jesus wasn't condemning this would-be disciple for having great wealth. *As an act of love*, he pointed out that his wealth was the most likely stumbling block that would eventually prevent him from experiencing everything God wanted to give him.

The importance of viewing **Surrender** in the context of love is likely why Jesus's strongest **Instruction** on counting the incredibly high cost of discipleship (Luke 14:27–35) is followed immediately by his three strongest parables concerning the love and care of our Father God (Luke 15:1–32). We can **Surrender** any desire, possession, or relationship and even take up a cross of suffering because—like a shepherd looking for a lost sheep, a widow looking for a lost coin, and a father looking day after day for the return of a lost son—we serve a loving God who is always looking to give up everything for us.

The Cost of Discipleship

Few followers of Jesus have marked out the expedition camp of **Surrender** as courageously as German theologian and activist Dietrich Bonhoeffer (1906–45). Born to wealth, Bonhoeffer shocked his family when he was fourteen years old by announcing Jesus had called him into ministry. He made good on his calling, completing a doctorate in theology, serving as assistant pastor of a church in Barcelona, and spending a year as an exchange student and lecturer in New York City.

Disappointed by what he thought was the shallow theology of Union Theological Seminary's faculty and students, Bonhoeffer accepted the invitation of a Black classmate, Frank Fisher, to attend the seven-thousand-member Abyssinian Baptist Church in Harlem. Here, at last, Bonhoeffer found Christians who took theology seriously. In fact, the preaching of African American pastor Adam Clayton Powell as well as the vitality of the Abyssinian congregation challenged Bonhoeffer's entire understanding of the kingdom of God. For the first time in his life, he found himself in relationship with marginalized and oppressed people who taught him the theology and practices of racial and economic justice.[5] As Reggie Williams details, "He encountered the Black Christ who suffered with African Americans in a White supremacist world [and] took that identity of the Black Christ with him when he returned to Nazi Germany."[6]

Bonhoeffer's return to Germany, just as Adolf Hitler rose to power, put his new ideals to the test. The overwhelming majority of Germany's Christian leaders kowtowed to Hitler. They refused to speak out against Nazism in general and anti-Semitism in particular, and not without reason. Soon Hitler grew so powerful even the Pope signed a deal agreeing not to criticize Hitler in exchange for a promise he would spare the Catholic Church.

Thanks to his experience in Harlem, Bonhoeffer could see the rising German nationalism as a compromise of the life and teachings of Jesus. Bonhoeffer leveraged his prestigious lectureship at the University of Berlin to publicly oppose Hitler. When Hitler came to power, Bonhoeffer took to the radio to denounce him. When Hitler banned Bonhoeffer from the airwaves, Bonhoeffer published "The Church and the Jewish Question," arguing that Nazism was an illegitimate form of government and therefore must be opposed on Christian grounds. He insisted that Jesus's command to love your neighbor as yourself demands that Christians fight evil by questioning the unjust practices of the state and helping all victims of injustice—be they Christian or Jew. True disciples must choose "not only to help the victims who have fallen under the wheel, but to fall into the spokes of the wheel itself" in order to halt the machinery of injustice.[7]

His words proved prophetic. When offered the opportunity to remain in the United States at the beginning of World War II, Bonhoeffer caught the last transatlantic ship leaving for Europe. Taking up his cross, he wrote a friend, "I will have no right to participate in the reconstruction of Christian life in Germany after the war if I do not share the trials of this time with my people."[8]

Once home, he used his pulpit to condemn Nazism. When the Nazis banned him from preaching, he wrote books. When Hitler banned him from publishing, he led an underground seminary. When the Nazis closed the seminary, Bonhoeffer joined the resistance movement, helping Jews escape Europe.

Eventually, Bonhoeffer paid dearly for his resistance to Hitler: first with his freedom and ultimately with his life. Implicated in a resistance movement attempt to assassinate Hitler, he was imprisoned in concentration camps with the same Jews he sought to defend. In April 1945, Nazis executed Bonhoeffer by a special order of the German high command just hours before Allied soldiers freed the concentration camp where he was being held.

Before he died, Bonhoeffer penned perhaps the world's greatest treatise on following the life and teachings of Jesus, *The Cost of Discipleship*. He devotes much of the work to parsing out the difference between what he calls "cheap grace" and "costly grace." With his life and words, he wrote:

> Cheap grace is grace without discipleship, grace without the cross, grace without the living, incarnate Jesus Christ. Costly grace is the hidden treasure in the field, for the sake of which people go and sell with joy everything they have . . . because the life of God's Son was not too costly for God to give in order to make us live.[9]

The Model of True Surrender

Bonhoeffer's life reminds us that Jesus never called his disciples (or us) to climb any higher into the death zone than he was willing to go himself. As you read the Gospel accounts of Jesus in the garden of Gethsemane, you can almost hear Jesus gasping for spiritual breath as he gazed up at the summit of the cross.

> STEP—gasp, gasp, gasp, gasp
> "My soul is overwhelmed with sorrow
> to the point of death . . ."
> FALL (on his face in prayer)—
> gasp, gasp, gasp, gasp
> "My Father, if it is possible,
> may this cup be taken from me"—
> gasp, gasp, gasp, gasp

> "Yet not as I will, but as you will."
> RISE (to find his disciples sleeping)—
> gasp,gasp, gasp, gasp
> REPEAT three times! (Matt. 26:38–45)

Unlike anyone else before or since, Jesus loved his heavenly Father and us with all his heart, soul, mind, and strength. As Lee Camp reminds us, he deliberately rejected the "expected modes of being Messiah and chose the way of the Suffering Servant."[10] And out of his love, he is willing to patiently and relentlessly root out any lesser **Desire** that will prevent our faith from growing to fruitful maturity. As Bonhoeffer discovered, those who understand what exchanging our lesser desires for what Jesus's kingdom desires for us will joyfully **Surrender** everything they have to purchase the buried treasure of God's love.

Even if that **Surrender** is often preceded by a nasty fall. (Gasp, gasp, gasp.)

A Climbing Guide for the Disciple's Ascent into
SURRENDER

There is nothing easy about the process of **Surrender**. Here is a spiritual practice that helps me.

First, Only, Now Questions

One practice that helps me take stock of where Jesus may be pushing upon an area of **Surrender** in my life is asking myself three questions and then journaling my answers.

1. *What am I seeking* First: Before All Else? This is primarily a schedule question. What is the one thing that never gets pushed out of your schedule each day? This shows the things you are already intrinsically motivated to do. Don't write "brushing my teeth" or "eating lunch"—just activities more particular to your life.

It may take you a few tries to figure this out, but it should give you a sense of what you seek *before* all else.

2. *What am I seeking* Only: Besides All Else? This is more of a thought exercise. Think through all the people, possessions, activities, and so on, in your life. What would you keep if you had to give up everything in your life except for one thing? It may take you a few tries to figure this out, but if you do, you will have a sense of what you seek *besides* all else.

3. *What am I seeking* Now: Beneath All Else? This is more of a daydreaming question. Set the alarm on your phone to go off every fifteen minutes. Each time it goes off, immediately send yourself a text recording whatever it was you were thinking about at that moment. By the end of the day, you will have a sense of what you seek *beneath* all else.

Jesus first; Jesus only; Jesus now—before, besides, and beneath all else. Once you understand the rivals for God's love that dwell within your soul, you can begin to bring them into the light of Jesus's loving gaze and **Surrender** them in exchange for his kingdom **Desires** for you.

Palms Up / Palms Down Prayer

One way to participate in this Surrender is with a prayer practice known as Palms Up / Palms Down. It goes like this.

Palms Up: Sit comfortably in a quiet place. Put your hands in your lap with your palms *up*, then pray, "Lord, your Word says that I can only truly love you as I experience your love. Please open 'the eyes of my heart' to grasp how 'wide and long and high and deep is the love of Christ'" (Eph. 1:18; 3:18). Imagine the Lord filling your empty hands with his love for you. Each time a thought of his love comes to mind, cup your hands and lift them to your chest, pressing their truth into your open heart. (I know it sounds cheesy, but it works.)

Palms Down: Now put your hands back in front of you with your palms *down*, then pray, "Lord, I release my lesser loves to you—my **Desires** for family, friends, fortune, fame, future, and anything that serves only my self-interest." Sit quietly with your palms down. Then, make a fist and allow the Lord to bring a particular rival of your love for him to mind—one you are holding on to. Each time one comes to mind, open your fist and drop them into the hands of God's loving care. Pray, "Lord, I release my attachment to this lesser love." You might want to cycle through this process a few times. Start doing this for just a few minutes each day, perhaps at the beginning or end of the day. You can build up to more time if this practice proves meaningful. And remember, these rivals for God's love are rarely *evil* **Desires**. They are merely *disordered* **Desires**. Once they are entrusted to God's care, they lose their hold on us. Once properly ordered, God can often return them to us full of his new purpose.

This Is My Surrender

While my journey of **Surrender** never approached the level sacrifice of Jesus or even Bonhoeffer, my first attempts at Palms Up / Palms Down may prove instructive for those starting on their Jesus Climb.

At the end of my junior year, I was selected to serve as president of my fellowship group. It didn't exactly fall into my lap. I desperately wanted the position. After all, the role of a Christian leader is the best way to help change the world for good, right? So, I waged a relentless campaign of attending every meeting, staying late, setting up chairs, and being an impressive (yet humble) Christian. And my efforts paid off. I was named president to the applause of all. Which was exactly what I really wanted. My **Desire** to be affirmed as a leader was a disordered one that now rivaled my love for God. As my anxiety diminished in other areas of my life, it began to manifest in a new way by generating a "false self" who felt safe only when he was in control. And who has more control than the leader of a group? Rather than loving others as Jesus taught his leaders in training, my leadership became an extension of my self-centered love. As Steve Cuss warns, "Leadership Anxiety is a sign that the false self is demanding we nourish it instead of dying to it."[11]

Jesus knew this, of course, and graciously began to work to get me to exchange my lesser love for kingdom love. As a poster child for "emotionally unhealthy discipleship,"[12] it didn't take long for people to notice that our fellowship group was becoming less and less about helping members walk with Jesus and more and more about making me look good. In just three months under my leadership, our fellowship group grew from *seventy* students all they way up to *seven*. (Yes, you read that right.)

Things came to a head during our last meeting before Christmas break. I became so frustrated with group members goofing off during Bible study (which reflected poorly on me as a "Christian leader") that I screamed at them, threw my Bible on the floor, and stormed out of the room. (I know. I know.) Our staff director, Tom, came and found me in the hallway and gently suggested, "Maybe it would be a good idea for you to step down as president?"

I had to agree.

Create in Me a Clean Heart

Full of shame, I spent my Christmas break far from God and most of my Christian friends. Mostly I listened to my Dementors wail things like, "You will never be a Christian leader. You are such a failure. You are defective. How could even God love you?" Night after night, I waited until my family went to bed and then sneaked into the quiet living room to stoke the fire in the hearth and pray for forgiveness. They didn't start as healthy prayers. My shame and self-condemnation were eating me alive.

Praying Palms Up / Palms Down (okay, mostly Palms Down) night after night helped awaken me to my true **Desires**. Slowly, I saw how I wasn't seeking Jesus *First*, *Only*, or *Now* in my first foray into Christian leadership. I was merely using Jesus as a means to *my* end. With a heart damaged by my parents' conditional love, my **Desire** was for any affirmation I could earn for my accomplishments—even "Christian leader" accomplishments—to make me feel worthy of being loved.

Only I didn't need to earn his love. As I meditated on God's love and forgiveness, Jesus reoriented my life with his teachings to see something I had never seen before. God doesn't love me because Jesus died for me; Jesus died for me *because* God loves me! Waking up to God's love brought me to a place of genuine **Surrender**. I wrote in my journal:

> Lord, thank you for your unbreakable love and your unimaginable forgiveness. I want to know you more than I've ever wanted anything in my whole life. . . . You're my only desire. Come take me and shape me into the image of your Son. I purpose to go back to every person in the group and to the group as a whole and confess my sin. I know they might refuse to forgive me. I might even lose all my friends. It's okay if people lose confidence in me. Just don't let them lose confidence in you.

Servant

When the New Year dawned, I returned to our youth group. Only this time, I came not as a leader but as a servant. Confessing my failure was tough. But my friends forgave me. It proved to be one of the most healing experiences of my life.

And guess what? Our fellowship group started to grow again. (Which was a little tough on my ego.) Soon we were back to seventy students and more.

Of course, Jesus is such a great Teacher that he scheduled a review session so that I wouldn't forget this lesson. During my graduation open house, he prompted dozens of friends to seek me out to tell me what a difference I had made in their life—each one named something I did to serve them *after* I stepped down as president.

Jesus had led me into the death zone, and I had fallen, badly! Yet he never stopped loving me. This is the beauty of surrender. We **Surrender** to **Love**.

*Scan the QR code below for the backstory on Gary's climb toward **Surrender**.*

FOUR

COMMUNITY

When Pillows Attack

"From this time many of his disciples turned back and no longer followed him. 'You do not want to leave too, do you?' Jesus asked the Twelve. Simon Peter answered him, 'Lord, to whom shall we go? You have the words of eternal life. We have come to believe and to know that you are the Holy One of God.'"

—John 6:66–69

While the 1953 British Everest expedition renewed their nation's efforts to climb the world's tallest mountain, an eight-man American mountaineering team set out to climb the world's second-highest peak, known as K2. While K2 stands nearly 750 feet shorter than Everest, most climbers consider its jagged 28,251-foot peak considerably more challenging. After months of planning, climbing, and acclimatization, the American team finally found themselves within sight of their goal. Then, just as they entered the death zone, a team member developed life-threatening blood clots in his legs. Pressing their heads together so they could hear one another above the hurricane roar of a raging snowstorm, team members made the agonizing decision to turn back. Tragedy struck on their descent.

A team member fell. In the white-out conditions, the next climber on the rope didn't realize what had happened until he too was pulled off his feet. Soon, a chain reaction led to one team member after another losing their footing and plunging uncontrollably toward the edge of the mountain.

Everyone would have died that day save for two life-altering factors. First, the entire team was bound together by a nearly unbreakable rope. Second, that rope was attached to Peter Schoening. In the brief moments it took his altitude-muddled brain to comprehend that everyone on his climbing team was hurtling down the mountain, Schoening quickly calculated that the momentum of five climbers falling at once would generate enough force to rip him from the mountain to join his teammates in certain death.

Instead of cutting the rope to save himself, Schoening used one hand to wrap it tightly around his shoulders. Then with his other hand he drove his ice axe deep into a crag between two boulders. He threw himself to ground just in time to absorb the full force of five grown men hurtling down the mountainside at close to forty miles per hour. The impact nearly tore Schoening in half. Yet, against all odds, his makeshift belay held. Somehow, he managed to arrest the fall of his entire team, saving them from certain death.

Known in the mountaineering world as the "Miracle Belay," alpinists regard Schoening's feat as the single most remarkable achievement in climbing history. (His ice axe hangs on display in the Bradford Washburn American Mountaineering Museum in Golden, Colorado.) Schoening's team discovered one of the most incontrovertible maxims of mountaineering: no climber is stronger than his team. Mountaineers adhere to a large variety of often contradictory climbing philosophies and techniques, yet one rule runs through every approach: "Never climb alone."

With Him

The ascent of genuine discipleship carries a similar warning. This is likely why Jesus spent an entire night in prayer before choosing his climbing partners—known as "the Twelve" (Luke 6:12). Mark tells us that he appointed the Twelve, first and foremost, that they might be "with him" (3:14).

Don't miss the simplicity of the statement. Mark wants to communicate to us that Jesus was so committed to not climbing solo that he deliberately roped himself to flawed climbing partners who could support him on his journey of ascent toward the cross. We often miss this aspect of Jesus's life. We are so biased toward seeing him as divine we often ignore his humanity, including his very human need for **Community**. Mark's Gospel emphasizes this point by placing Jesus's selection of the Twelve just before one of the most emotionally charged conflicts in Jesus's life. First, Jesus's family in Nazareth grows so anxious and embarrassed by his behavior that they decide "he is out of his mind" and leave for Capernaum "to take charge of him" (3:21). Then, while his family is on their way, the nation's religious leaders arrive on the scene from Jerusalem and pronounce Jesus as "possessed by Beelzebul . . . the prince of demons" (3:22).

Imagine how you might feel if your family wanted to commit you to a psychiatric facility while your professors were declaring you demon possessed on CNN. Then remember that Jesus, while fully God, is also 100 percent a human being capable of being tested in every way we are (Heb. 4:15). Now, imagine if at this exact moment your family arrived on campus and came to your 10:00 a.m. history class to take you away by force. Jesus must now choose not only between his brothers and the kingdom of God but also between his saintly mother and his calling.

How does Jesus keep climbing amid such deeply personal opposition? **Community**. Mark tells us that the crowd in the house where he was teaching told him, "Your mother and brothers are outside looking for you" (3:32).

"'Who are my mother and my brothers?' [Jesus] asked. Then he looked at those seated in a circle around him and said, 'Here are my mother and my brothers!'" (3:33–34).

It was those seated in the circle around him—the Twelve and likely the other students traveling with him—who gave him the strength to go on. He had roped himself to the Twelve that they might be "with him," and now in his hour of need, their presence with him gave Jesus the strength he needed to continue climbing. I am not saying Jesus would have failed without the help of his climbing community. There's a mystery to Jesus's divine/human nature and mission far too deep to explore here. However, I am saying he modeled a commitment to **Community** without which his *disciples* clearly would have failed. If Jesus chose to rope himself to climbing partners, how can we expect to climb to genuine discipleship without following his example?

Spiritual Belay

Perhaps no event in Jesus's ministry better illustrates this reality than Peter's heroics in John's Gospel. Let me map it out for you.

First, Jesus feeds a crowd of more than five thousand men, women, and children in the wilderness on the far side of the Sea of Galilee (John 6:1–13).

Second, seeing this miracle, the crowd (correctly) concludes that Jesus must be "the prophet" promised by Moses[1] and then (incorrectly) attempts to make Jesus king by force (6:14–15).

Third, Jesus refuses their election results, hides himself on top of a mountain, then sifts his students' faith by walking on the surface of the water on his way across the Sea of Galilee (6:16–24).

Fourth, when the crowd finds Jesus in Capernaum, Jesus **Instructs** them that their lesser **Desires** for earthly food and a political king must be **Surrendered** and exchanged for his kingdom by partaking of him, the bread of life (6:25–59).

This is too much for many followers. Finally, just like the rich young ruler, the crowd not only grumbles about Jesus's teaching; they reject him as their Teacher. John the Beloved tells us: "From this time many of his disciples turned back and no longer followed him" (6:60–66).

Avalanche

Avalanches are responsible for nearly one-third of all deaths on Mount Everest. In this critical moment on the spiritual journey, it is easy to see how Jesus's students must have felt themselves caught up in this avalanche of unbelief. Imagine being one of the Twelve that day. In less than twenty-four hours, you have gone from witnessing one of the greatest miracles of all time, resulting in the crowd trying to crown Jesus as king, to Jesus chasing away the very same crowd—including many if not most of his disciples—by challenging them with difficult teachings.

What's worse, Jesus doesn't even seem concerned by these developments. He does not run after the crowd with more "consumer-friendly" admissions materials or robocall the students who transferred out of his program offering them a more watered-down gospel. Instead, Jesus simply watches these disciples walk away, then calmly turns to the Twelve and asks, "You do not want to leave too, do you?" (6:67).

You can almost see the spiritual chain reaction as Jesus's students begin to lose their discipleship footing and start plunging uncontrollably toward the edge of unbelief. It is entirely possible that their spiritual journeys would have ended that day, if not for two life-altering factors: First, Jesus had roped his disciples together with the unbreakable cord of **Community**. Second, they had Simon Peter on their rope team.

Driving his spiritual ice axe between the boulders of their shared belief and the glacial ice of their shared experience, Peter speaks not just for himself but for his entire climbing team, "Lord, to whom shall we go? You have the words of eternal life. We have come to believe and to know that you are the Holy One of God" (6:68–69).

Together!

This is Peter's "Miracle Belay." Just like his great confession in the synoptic Gospels (Matt. 16:16; Mark 8:29; Luke 9:20), Peter speaks as the mouthpiece for his entire **Community**. This is not a cop-out on the part of the other disciples; it is the way our faith works in tandem with the faith of others. This is how we make our faith our own . . . together.

Getting baptized or praying a prayer to receive Christ is not the final act in the story of someone's Christian discipleship, it is merely the end of Act I. It is the place where the hero puts aside their old **Desires** and crosses the Rubicon by declaring their commitment to the quest of following Jesus up the mountain of discipleship. But if the Gospels teach us anything, it is that such fledgling "belief" is not the same thing as the mature faith of the final act. In fact, like the disciples who turn back in John 6, it may not be true faith at all.

This makes **Community** crucial to genuine discipleship. **Community** is the place where we look to those seated in the circle around us to publicly confirm and rehearse the commitments we have made as individuals. **Community** helps us remain rooted in who we truly are, or maybe better put, who we *aspire* to be. Not a false self we put on like a mask to posture before the world—pretending to have more faith than we really possess when we're around our Christian friends, then pretending our faith isn't that important to us when around our non-Christian friends. In **Community**, we can begin to become our true selves as we rope our lives to friends and mentors who accept us for who we are, affirm our strengths, help us remain authentic about our weaknesses, and hold us accountable to our spiritual aspirations.

The Power of a Climbing Community

Few disciples in American history modeled the power of **Community** as remarkably as chemist Mary Lyon (1797–1849), founder of Mount Holyoke College. Born to a struggling Massachusetts farming family, Lyon's profound intellect and spiritual passion might have easily succumbed to the tragedy of losing her father to death at age five and her mother to abandonment when Mary was only thirteen.[2] God often proves his power in our weakness, and Lyon's lack of parental presence taught her to bind herself to others with the ropes of **Community**. Local families provided her room and board so she could attend classes in town during the week, and her older brother's family provided shelter each weekend. Mary later told her students, "My father and mother forsook me, but the Lord took me up."[3]

Mary's academic achievements became the talk of Sanderson Academy, where trustees offered her a full-tuition scholarship, wondering, "What matter of woman . . . could learn the Latin Grammar in three days?"[4] Soon, Lyon's remarkable "solidity of mind" and "power of humorous description" prompted a local village to invite her to serve as their summer schoolteacher.[5] At first, her students resented having a seventeen-year-old teach them. But over time, Mary won them over, proving the metal of her lifetime motto: "If you commence teaching, and do not succeed, teach till you do succeed."[6]

The experience convinced Lyon of her need for further training. So, she devoted her next years to education. She fell in love with the sciences at Amherst Academy, where she studied chemistry and botany with legendary laboratory scientist Amos Eaton.[7] She continued her summer teaching to support herself, even earning teaching roles at schools with male-only faculty policies.[8] Lyon's hunger for learning eventually led her to the women's school with the most robust academic reputation—Byfield Women's Seminary. Headmaster Joseph Emerson was a strong champion of women's education and rigorous academic training. He also imbued Lyon with a love for the theology and practices of the New Divinity movement. New Divinity ministers emphasized reliance on prayer for the Holy Spirit to "intensify and accelerate" his usual work during seasons of revival[9] capable of converting each new generation of students as well as the belief that the only true sign of genuine conversion was a life of other-centered love.[10] From that point forward, "self-sacrificial benevolence . . . became the guiding principle of her life."[11]

Lyon's keen intellect, quiet spirituality, and commitment to **Community** drew the attention of Byfield's assistant principal, Zilpah Grant (Banister). Like Barnabas recognizing the brilliance of the apostle Paul,[12] Grant took Lyon under her wing, serving as both an instructor and an advocate. The two educators roped their lives together in a friendship that bore a hundredfold fruit in promoting women's education and foreign missions. Together, Grant and Lyon guided numerous women's seminaries toward spiritual and intellectual renewal.

Their lifework culminated in 1837 when—much like Barnabas and Paul—Mary stepped into the leadership role. In an era when women's seminaries were often little more than finishing schools for marriageable young women with curricula filled with dance and social graces, Mary envisioned a school distinguished by the academic rigor of Byfield's Emerson, the scientific inquiry of Amherst's Eaton, and the spiritual vitality of the New Divinity. This vision became reality in Lyon founding Mount Holyoke Women's Seminary in South Hadley, Massachusetts. Lyon and Grant's deep reliance on **Community** made this unusual interweaving of educational elements possible.

Having spent a lifetime roping themselves to their students, their students' mothers, and the women of the New Divinity movement prayer circles, Mary proposed founding a women's college not upon the fickle philanthropy of a few wealthy male benefactors but by "crowdsourcing" women. Mary crisscrossed New England, raising pennies at a time. Her first "major gift" of one thousand dollars[13] came not from a wealthy male benefactor but the combined offerings of the women's prayer and knitting circles in Ipswich, Massachusetts. Having roped themselves to these women, Lyon and Grant now experienced the strength of their belay.[14]

Lyon's second **Community**-based educational innovation stemmed from her deep commitment to keeping a Mount Holyoke education within the financial means of middle- and low-income students (like her younger self). Decades before the founding of America's first official "work colleges," Lyon organized Mount Holyoke students to do the work of their school to keep tuition low. Rather than hiring (expensive) male teachers like most women's seminaries, Mary drew upon the best of her and Grant's former students. Rather than hiring a male campus minister, students led the daily "neighborhood prayer meetings," making revivals—eleven in twelve years—"more common and numerous at the seminary than at any other institution of higher education."[15]

Lyon's third educational innovation was to reproduce her missional **Community** relationship with Grant in the lives of her students. She fearlessly focused Mount Holyoke's mission upon educating women willing to serve in other-centered benevolence as teachers throughout rural America and around the world. A woman making a lifetime commitment to foreign missions was unknown in Lyon's day, yet "no other institution was as closely associated with women missionaries as Mount Holyoke."[16] By the time Lyon died in 1849, thirty-five Mount Holyoke women had embraced Lyon's call to go to the nations. By 1885, one-fifth of all American female missionaries were Holyoke alums.[17] Then in 1886, Robert Wilder, brother of Mount Holyoke student Grace Wilder, used the mission covenant created by Grace's prayer group—*I purpose, God willing, to become a foreign missionary*—to launch the Student Volunteer Movement (SVM).[18] In the end, over thirty thousand students took the Mount Holyoke pledge, with nearly twelve thousand reaching the foreign mission field (roughly half of them women), making the SVM the largest foreign missions movement in US history.[19]

Ten years after Lyon's death, Dr. Edward Hitchcock (1793–1864), the president of Amherst College, declared, "I do not mean that Miss Lyon had attained to Christian perfection; but, were anyone to assert that such a grace was hers, I confess that my memory could bring no facts to refute the claim."[20] Lyon personally taught more than three thousand students, revolutionized higher education, and helped launch nearly ten thousand women into careers as teachers motivated by other-centered benevolence.[21]

Lyon credited her success to the **Community** she shared with her lifelong climbing partnership with Grant. She urged her students, "Some suppose the strength of affection is greater in youth than in advanced life. This may be true of worldly love, but not of Christian love. Do you not think I can and do love Miss Grant more than when we [began]? You need not fear loving too ardently, if you only love in Christ. . . . Young ladies, I want you to love so deeply . . . that the roots will strike into your inmost souls."[22]

Lyon and Grant learned the secret of *ascending* into genuine discipleship: our individual progress in **Desire, Instruction,** and **Surrender** to Jesus and his kingdom is intricately connected to the **Community** of climbers to whom we rope ourselves. They spent their lives urging their students to form communities of faith capable of helping each climbing partner continue on their Jesus Climb through all the ups and downs of their journey. Genuine **Community** forges an unbreakable bond for our journey toward the summit of genuine discipleship, even though individually we are far from perfect.

Conflict

Of course, this is where our problem starts. **Community** always sounds great *in theory*. Who wouldn't want to have a close group of friends, teammates, and climbing partners? But let's be honest, the strongest argument against **Community** is **Community**. The closer we grow to others, the more conflict we experience. Commit yourself to a **Community**—be it a climbing team, a friend, a spouse, a neighborhood, or a church—and sooner or later they will disappoint, abandon, or betray you. Conflict is central to the human experience, even among humans who aspire to love as Jesus did. As the Irish toast goes: "To live above, with saints we love, oh that will be glory. But to live below, with the saints we know? Now that's a different story!"

Yet interpersonal conflict seems to be one of the primary reasons why Jesus built his college on face-to-face interaction in live-fire **Community**. Meeting asynchronously with online students in a one-on-one learning system would have proven significantly easier for him. But it would not produce the transformational learning environment he desired. He wanted his students to become genuine disciples capable of loving one another with the same sacrificial mindset he employed in loving them (John 13:34).

The learning **Community** Jesus established served both as a greenhouse for bringing out the best in his disciples and as a crucible for revealing the worst in them. **Community** affirms our greatest strengths and confronts us with our greatest weaknesses. **Community** is where we learn the relational arts of not judging, not competing, not seeking our own interests, and not pointing out the speck in another's eye before dealing with the plank in our own.

Jesus was not some dewy-eyed idealist. He chose his climbing team knowing full well that one of them would betray him to his death and that everyone would eventually abandon him in his hour of greatest need. So, he taught his disciples that no **Community** can flourish beyond its members' ability to forgive one another. When Peter complained to Jesus, "How many times shall I forgive my brother or sister who sins against me? Up to seven times?" Jesus answered him, "I tell you, not seven times, but seventy-seven times" (Matt. 18:21–22). Jesus wants the measure of forgiveness we extend to others to match the Lord's forgiveness of our offenses. Nothing restores relationships quite like the words, "I forgive you." Nothing helps restore broken trust quite like the words, "I was wrong. What can I do to make things right?" In other words, like nearly every element of genuine discipleship, **Community** grows only by hard work!

A Climbing Guide for the Disciple's Ascent into
COMMUNITY

How do we grow in our commitment to **Community**? Two spiritual practices have greatly helped me. The first is rather obvious: choosing a strong climbing team.

Choosing a Climbing Team

Expert mountain climbers have found that the ideal climbing partners and teams possess six crucial characteristics. They not only correlate well with Jesus's training of his disciples but also make a good checklist for finding **Community** climbing partners today.

1. *A strong commitment to summiting.* Mountaineers want team members who desperately desire to make it up the mountain and are willing to make the painful sacrifices necessary to get there. Jesus appears to have chosen climbing partners who were the most spiritually hungry among the crowds who followed him.

Who do you know who seems hungry to grow spiritually and "go for the summit" of kingdom love? Don't worry if they're a long-term believer or just beginning to explore following Jesus as their teacher. You can belay one another on the journey.

2. *An equally strong commitment to teammates.* Team leaders also seek climbing partners as committed to their teammates as they are to the climb; team members willing to risk their own lives when a teammate is in danger. Jesus taught his disciples that he wanted climbing partners who were willing to be servants of all and, like him, willing to lay down their lives for their teammates.

Who do you know who seems to be committed to helping *others* grow spiritually?

3. *Proven knot-tying and rope-management abilities.* Mountaineers also search for team members gifted in the skills of making

every knot secure and keeping every rope untangled. Jesus spent much of his time not only teaching his students about the importance of tying the knots of loving one another but also training them in rope management whenever they tangled their lines of communication (normally by arguing over who would have the greatest place of honor in the coming kingdom). They needed to learn how to wash one another's feet like their master.

Who do you know who seems to be good at building strong relationships?

4. *Unusual belaying skill.* Team leaders want climbers like Peter Schoening, who possess extensive experience in the techniques of supporting and, when necessary, carrying their teammates in difficult and varied situations. Clearly, Simon Peter possessed the belaying skills necessary to catch his climbing mates. Yet his fellow disciples weren't so bad either. Jesus had roped them together in such a way that no less than seven different disciples spoke up at least eleven different times during their final evening together (Matt. 26:17–29; Mark 14:12–25; Luke 22:7–38; John 13–16).

Who do you know who seems committed to supporting others and even carrying them in difficult situations?

5. *Long-term relationships.* Team leaders seek to build teams with a critical mass of climbers who know each other well and have climbed together often. Jesus built the core of his climbing team around two sets of brothers—Peter and Andrew, James and John—who had known each other and even worked together in their family fishing business their entire lives. Is there anyone you've listed above that you seem to be already committed to in some way? Maybe someone on your sports team, choir, workplace, or even just where you live.

6. *Diverse experience.* Mountaineers strive to make sure their team is composed of climbers of diverse experiences and backgrounds, as research demonstrates that the more diversity a

climbing team possesses the better decisions they make and the less likely they are to make poor decisions due to "group think." Jesus deliberately included climbing partners as diverse as Simon the Zealot, committed to overthrowing the Roman government, and Matthew the tax collector, who benefited from his close relationship with Rome.

Are there people you've listed above who challenge you to see things in new ways? Maybe someone from a different culture, friend group, or ethnicity. If not, add a few. Now, approach a few people (one is enough to start) whose names appear more than once in answer to the questions above. Pray for the opportunity to talk with them about becoming climbing partners.

Mike's Belay

What does that look like? Let me tell you what that looked like for me. I had a number of climbing partners in high school, but my first college climbing partner taught me a valuable lesson about roping myself to teammates different from me. Honestly, I wasn't sure what I thought of Mike when I first met him. He was, in his own words, a bit of a wild man. A convert from a life of drugs, his huge beard and intensely extroverted personality were just too much for me. He and a friend even dressed in buckskin for each home football game to stir up the crowd with their zany antics.

But after getting to know each other better, Mike became an important mentor in my life. Then one day he confided in me, "I know spending solitude time with God in prayer and biblical meditation are important, man, but college life is so darn busy, I keep pushing them out of my schedule."

"I can't believe you admitted that to me!" I replied. "I'm having the same problem!"

Mike twisted his beard and proposed the perfect strategy for a spiritual belay: "Let's do something about it together."

We looked at our schedules and realized neither of us had a nine a.m. class.

"Okay, we have a time," I said. "Where do we meet?"

"How 'bout the prayer chapel in the student union building?" Mike suggested. "It's close to both of our eight o'clock classes and to the ten o'clock chapel service."

So, we roped ourselves together to start meeting every Monday through Friday from nine to ten. And guess what? I didn't miss a single "quiet time" the entire semester . . . until midterms. That is when I learned the true power of **Community**.

After procrastinating on a major paper for my geology class, I had to pull an all-nighter to finish it. I submitted just in time for my eight a.m. class, then crashed into bed and the sweet oblivion of sleep . . . forgetting all about my commitment with Mike.

The details of what happened next are a little fuzzy, but somewhere around nine twenty, Mike burst through my door. Pulling my roommate's pillow off his empty bunk, he began to beat me with it, crying out, "Repent, you sinner. It is time to rise and seek the Lord. Repent!" Then he pushed me out of bed and onto the floor, stuck my Bible in my lap, and sat right next to me, close enough to elbow me each time I started nodding off. It was the worst quiet time of my life, but I learned an important lesson on the power of **Community**.

What about you? Do you have potential climbing partners in your life? Like Mike and I, rope yourself together by agreeing to a regular time and place to meet. Then hold each other accountable to meditate on and follow Jesus's teachings. If you can find a team leader—a mentor far enough ahead on their spiritual journey to help guide your climbing team—that's all the better. However, it should not be a requirement. If Jesus gave such care to the selection and training of his climbing partners, do we really have any hope of summiting the heights of genuine discipleship without following his example?

Forgiveness at the Lord's Table

Of course, even Jesus didn't pick a perfect team, which is why we need to employ the second spiritual practice of forgiveness. Shortly before he began his journey to the cross, Jesus transformed the simple act of eating a meal together into a profound spiritual experience:

> While they were eating, Jesus took bread, and when he had given thanks, he broke it and gave it to his disciples, saying, "Take and eat; this is my body [given for you; do this in remembrance of me]."
>
> Then he took a cup, and when he had given thanks, he gave it to them, saying, "Drink from it, all of you. This is my blood of the [new] covenant, which is poured out for many for the forgiveness of sins." [And they all drank from it.] (Matt. 26:26–28; with Mark 14:23 and Luke 22:19–20)

Over the centuries since, Christians have disagreed on the precise theological meaning of Jesus's **Instruction** to partake of the bread and drink together. "Low church" traditions believe *every* meal Jesus's followers eat together should include an element of remembering Jesus in the breaking of bread. "High church" traditions believe the only true celebration of Communion takes place when a church gathers for a formal worship service.

What we do know for certain is that Jesus intended the celebration of "the Lord's Table" to be a *regular* practice in the **Community** of his followers.[23] The celebration of remembering his body given for us, and celebration of his blood poured out for the forgiveness of sins. As Henri Nouwen declares, "*Forgiveness* and *celebration* are what make a **Community**, whether a marriage, a friendship, or any other form of community."[24]

This makes the regular rhythm of the celebration of the Lord's Table a wonderful context for the practice of seeking and extending forgiveness to our imperfect climbing teams. In the Sermon on the Mount, Jesus instructed his disciples to reflect on their treatment of one another beyond mere outward obedience to the law. The question is not whether or not we have murdered someone in our **Community**, but have we been guilty of hatred, anger, or belittling others? Jesus then directed his followers, "Therefore, if you are offering your gift at the altar and there remember that your brother or sister has something against you, leave your gift there in front of the altar. First go and be reconciled to them; then come and offer your gift" (Matt. 5:23–24).

Jesus clearly expects his disciples to quickly ask forgiveness from those they've wronged and quickly forgive others who have wronged them.[25] Using the occasion of celebrating the Lord's Table together to practice asking forgiveness from anyone we have wronged strengthens the **Community** of Jesus's disciples. The Lord's Table provides the perfect context for the regular practice of reflecting on our love of neighbor and, when necessary, speaking the words, "I was wrong. I hope you can find it in your heart to forgive." No **Community** is stronger than its members' ability to forgive and ask forgiveness. No **Community** we build is stronger than our willingness to belay one another to faith in times of weakness and doubt. We make our faith our own . . . together.

*Scan the QR code below for the backstory on Gary's climb toward **Community**.*

PART TWO

DESCENT

The disciple's *descent* into a deeper and deeper experience of the intimate, transforming, and other-centered love of God.

FIVE

INTIMACY

A Damnable Heresy

"Blessed are you, Simon son of Jonah, for this was not revealed to you by flesh and blood, but by my Father in heaven."

—Jesus of Nazareth (Matt. 16:17)

George Mallory discovered the first secret to summiting Everest—acclimatization—purely by accident. However, Mallory's role in the second secret to summiting Everest was far more intentional. The failure of the 1921 expedition renewed debate as to whether humans could survive in the death zone long enough to make the summit. So, in preparation for the 1922 British expedition, the Royal Geographical Society enlisted the help of eminent Austrian physical chemist George Ingle Finch to develop a device by which Mallory's team members could supplement their lung capacity by breathing bottled oxygen during their climb.[1]

At first, Mallory considered supplemental oxygen "a damnable heresy" against the sporting nature of mountaineering. Not to mention the fact that he feared the added weight of lugging cumbersome tanks up the mountain would prove detrimental to a successful climb. However, after experiencing Everest's death zone firsthand, Mallory changed his tune. In a letter home to his wife, Ruth, just before his final ascent, Mallory wrote:

> It has always been my pet plan to climb the mountain gasless [without supplemental oxygen]. . . . Still, the conquest of the mountain is the great thing . . . and the gas will give me, perhaps, the best chance of all of getting to the top.[2]

Whether or not Mallory and his climbing partner, Andrew "Sandy" Irvine, made it to the summit that day remains the greatest mystery in mountaineering history. We know that at 12:50 p.m., teammate Noel Odell caught a brief glimpse of the pair successfully climbing one of the final cliffs on their route to the summit. However, Odell's sighting was the last anyone saw of either climber until the discovery of Mallory's body seventy-five years later. Since it was impossible to tell if Mallory had fallen on their ascent or descent, many refuse to believe he and Irvine reached the summit. Others point to recent circumstantial evidence and insist that they did, in fact, make it.[3] Since there is insufficient evidence to know for sure, the debate continues.

What is certain is that Mallory's conversion to the use of bottled oxygen remains one of his lasting legacies. From 1924 onward, each time mountaineers make their upward/downward climb into Everest's thin air, they carry an oxygen tank to store at the upper camps for their final push for the summit. Now, the climber's month-long preparation process not only enables their bodies to draw ten times more oxygen per breath, it also gives them a cache of oxygen tanks ready for use in the death zone. In other words, to successfully summit Everest, climbers require *both* the internal transformation provided by weeks of acclimatization *and* an external source of oxygen that enables them to climb beyond their natural abilities.[4]

Explicit Knowledge

It turns out bottled oxygen isn't such a bad metaphor for how Jesus led his first students into a deeper and deeper experience of the love and life of God. Bottled oxygen is not something the mountain climber "earns" or "develops." It is, by definition, "supplemental"—a gift from outside the climber designed to keep them alive on their journey to and from the summit. Each disciple's experience of God's life and love is remarkably similar.

First, God created human beings with at least two distinct "operating systems" for managing our understanding of the world. Explicit knowledge describes the operating system by which we amass and recombine ideas and practices into increasingly complex knowledge and skills. We have more or less direct control of this linear, logical, and language-based type of knowledge. It governs everything from how we process the information in a social media post to how we educate students.

For instance, a student in an anatomy and physiology class utilizes their explicit knowledge abilities to memorize the names and functions of seemingly countless human body parts to form an understanding of how the systems work together. While this process involves hard work and commitment, the outcomes are observable and measurable. Teachers can even assign an objective grade to this type of explicit knowledge acquisition. Any qualified student committed enough to focus their behavior on the skills required to master the information can earn a solid grade.

Explicit knowledge is a crucial element of a disciple's upward journey of ascent. As noted in the last four chapters, Jesus tells his students that those who refuse to master his teachings and grow in their commitment to following them "cannot be my disciples" (Luke 14:33; Matt. 7:21–27).

Experiential Knowledge

But is that all there is to following Jesus? It turns out God also created human beings with a second operating system: experiential knowledge. Experiential knowledge is not about managing information so much as managing our personal experiences and relationships with others. This implicit, or "gut level," knowledge involves the nonlinear, nonverbal, and holistic emotional connections that reach back as far as the womb.

Experiential knowledge controls most of our daily actions, especially our relationships with others, including God. Our brain processes experiential knowledge automatically before even consulting our explicit understanding. We instantly react to people and situations, feeling "in our gut" that someone or something is good or bad, right or wrong, without even thinking about it.

Experiential knowledge is programmed so deeply into our psyches that we just "know that we know that we know" something is true, even if it contradicts our professed explicit knowledge. For instance, if your childhood featured an untrustworthy father figure, you just know in your gut "fathers can't be trusted," so you automatically react with mistrust when encountering father figures, even when that father figure is the God you profess to worship with your explicit knowledge.[5]

This is why experiential knowledge is an essential aspect of the college of Jesus. In the same way that there is a difference between having a rational judgment that honey is sweet and having a sense of its sweetness, there is a profound difference between amassing explicit knowledge *about* God and experiencing God.[6] As theologian J. I. Packer warns, "One can know a great deal about God without much knowledge of him."[7]

Suppose your friend posts a photo of the fried-green-tomato omelet she is currently eating at a famous Southern restaurant with the caption, "Delicious!" Now, suppose you are much more of a foodie than your friend. You have already heard about this famous omelet. You may have read hundreds of reviews proclaiming it "delicious!" Perhaps you studied the restaurant's online menu and can list all the ingredients that make it so delicious. You may have even watched the omelet prepared by a famous chef on a cooking show, where she won a national award for its deliciousness.

Still, for all your explicit knowledge about the deliciousness of the omelet, your clueless, non-foodie friend who just tasted the omelet *knows* its deliciousness in a way that you don't. She understands it by experience. In the same way, Jesus wants his students to master more than just the recipes in his discipleship cookbook. He wants them to follow his **Instruction** and his example so they can cook up the experience of genuine discipleship. As the psalmist declares, "Taste and see that the LORD is good" (Ps. 34:8).

A Gift of Grace

This kind of experiential knowledge of God is the supplemental oxygen of the disciple's upward/downward journey. Peter and the Twelve did not know Jesus as the Holy One of God by their intelligence or efforts but because God "taught" them (John 6:44–45; Isa. 54:13). They were "drawn" to Jesus by the Father, who granted them the ability to know him (John 6:65). In other words, during their time in the college of Jesus, the Father had granted them the "bottled oxygen" grace they needed for this crucial moment in their faith journey.

The common definition of grace as "unmerited favor" stems from the apostle Paul's declaration, "For it is by grace you have been saved, through faith—and this is not from yourselves, it is the gift of God—not by works, so that no one can boast" (Eph. 2:8–9).

Much of the experience of the life and love of God each disciple carries up the mountain of their ascent into a higher and higher commitment to God is not something they have earned or even learned but rather something gifted to them by God.

For instance, Matthew tells us that after Peter made his "great confession" that Jesus is the Messiah, Jesus turned to him and declared: "Blessed are you, Simon son of Jonah, for this was not revealed to you by flesh and blood, but by my Father in heaven" (Matt. 16:17). Jesus was teaching his disciples that there are certain things that even the best disciple cannot "learn." It must be revealed (granted) to them by God. As one of my mentors once preached on this verse, "There is such a thing, as a spiritual and divine light, immediately imparted to the soul by God, of a different nature from any that is obtained by natural means."[8]

However, here is where the Sunday school definition of grace can steer us wrong. God's freely gifted and unearned grace is much more than mere "favor." Nor is it limited to the granting of forgiveness of sins and life eternal, as crucial as these may be. As John's Gospel tells us, Jesus came from the Father full of grace and truth, and out of this fullness, he brought grace upon grace. "For the law was given through Moses; grace and truth came through Jesus Christ. No one has ever seen God, but the one and only Son, who is himself God and is in closest relationship with the Father, has made him known" (John 1:14–18).

Grace is the revelation of God, the knowledge of God, the experience of God's love and forgiveness, as well as the fullness of the life of God acting in each disciple's life to accomplish what we cannot or will not do on our own. As Jesus tells his heavenly Father in his great High Priestly Prayer, "This is eternal life: that they *know* you, the only true God, and Jesus Christ, whom you have sent" (John 17:3—italics mine). The Greek word for "to know" (*ginosko*) in this verse means "to understand by experience." The

Hebrew version of "to know" (*yada'*) is so charged with relational meaning, biblical authors use it to denote sexual intimacy. As biblical scholars J. Scott Duvall and J. Daniel Hays explain, "It is impossible to even imagine discipleship or righteousness, as Jesus conceives it, apart from relational presence."[9]

Think back to Peter's "miracle belay" in the Gospel of John. When Jesus's "hard teaching" resulted in many of his students transferring out of his college, Jesus turned to the Twelve and asked if they wanted to transfer out as well. Peter responded, "To whom else shall we go? . . . We believe and have come to know you as the Holy One of God" (John 6:68–69 GDS). While many of Jesus's disciples began to follow him as students because they *believed* he was the Messiah, they turned back when Jesus took them into the death zone. The Twelve, however, were able to continue following Jesus because, in addition to their belief, they had also come to *know* him as the Holy One of God.[10]

Two Journeys, One Timeline

This points to the second reason the Sunday school definition of grace as "unmerited favor" misses something important. Just because Jesus's first students did not earn God's gracious revelation of the knowledge of his Son does not mean they did not seek it. As Dallas Willard was fond of saying, "Grace is not opposed to effort, but to earning."

Remember, our *ascent* into a higher and higher commitment and our *descent* into a deeper and deeper experience take place "at the same time." In the same way the right hand and left hand play distinct roles in a single piano concerto, the disciple's upward and downward journeys blend together to form a single masterpiece. The disciple's *descent* into an experiential knowledge of God and God's love provides the ability to continue their climb toward the summit of discipleship. At the same time, the disciple's *ascent* toward a higher and higher commitment to loving God with all their heart, soul, mind, and strength puts them in a position where the descent into a deeper experiential knowledge becomes possible. This is precisely what Jesus promised. "Those who hold to my teachings and follow them are the ones who truly love me; they will know the love of the Father, because I will reveal myself to them" (John 14:21 GDS).

This does not mean the disciple earns the grace of God nor that the grace of God forces the disciple to act. While the work of our timeless God always "precedes" human actions, Jesus teaches his students that his Father has granted them what seventeenth-century scientist and theologian Blaisé Pascal describes as "the dignity of causality." Learning and following Jesus's teachings and practices become the means by which grace enters the soul. In the same way that a surfer is incapable of catching the limitless power of ocean waves without a surfboard, the disciple who refuses to follow Jesus's teachings and way of life is incapable of catching the waves of God's boundless grace. Our seeking, obeying, learning, and practicing matter because they put us in a position to receive God's grace. As Ruth Haley Barton reminds us:

> I cannot transform myself, or anyone else for that
> matter. What I can do is create the conditions in which
> spiritual transformation can take place, by developing
> and maintaining a rhythm of spiritual practices that
> keep me open and available to God.[11]

Nowhere is this more evident in the journey of *descent* than in the practice of **Prayer**.

Prayer and Intimacy with God

Jesus refers to the fatherhood of God no less than sixteen times in the three chapters of the Sermon on the Mount (Matt. 5–7).

Even more incredibly, Jesus teaches his students to address God in prayer as their "Father," and even "Abba" (literally, "My own dear father"). Abba implies a close personal and familial relationship. As New Testament scholar Jim Dunn asserts, "What others thought too intimate in praying to God, Jesus used because of its intimacy."[12] As Singaporean theologian Simon Chan affirms, "Intimacy with God is what characterizes a life of prayer."[13]

And if the fatherhood of God is the heart of the Sermon on the Mount, then prayer is its circulatory system. Jesus mentions prayer in no less than fifteen verses, and nearly every one of those verses is somehow related to the Fatherly care of God. Jesus repeatedly reminds his students that his God is a loving, merciful, engaging, caring, attentive Father who knows their needs before they even ask and wants to grant them answers to their prayers. He even closes his teaching on prayer with a parable comparing the love of human fathers to divine love. "Which of you, if your son asks for bread, will give him a stone? Or if he asks for a fish, will give him a snake? If you, then, though you are evil, know how to give good gifts to your children, how much more will your Father in heaven give good gifts to those who ask him!" (Matt. 7:9–11).

A Soul Aflame for God

Teresa of Ávila (1515–82) offers a particularly helpful guide in the process of growing in **Intimacy** in our prayer life. Banished to a nunnery for a forbidden relationship at the age of sixteen, Teresa was astonished by how her soul took to a life of prayer. After more than twenty years of quiet prayer and horrific physical illnesses, supernatural experiences of spiritual intimacy "descended like a monsoon on the parched landscape of Teresa's soul."[14] As word of her remarkable God experiences spread throughout Spain, Teresa drew the attention of both the Spanish Inquisition, which sought to discredit her teaching, and spiritually hungry seekers (such as John of the Cross, discussed below) who sought her wisdom for fostering intimacy in prayer. In her spiritual autobiography, Teresa relates how she discovered that disciples often experience more than one type of intimacy with God in prayer.

In the first type, the Prayer of the Mind, we're like someone trying to get water out of the bottom of an open well with a leaky bucket. It is hard work training our minds to go back to focusing on the love of God again and again. In this stage it seems like there is very little **Intimacy** payoff for the effort expended. We often leave such times of prayer as thirsty to know God's love as we entered them.

In the second type, the Prayer of the Heart,[15] we're more like someone using a hand pump to bring up the subterranean water. The Holy Spirit guides our prayer efforts to move beyond knowing about God's love into maddeningly short bursts of knowing God's love experientially.

In the third type, the Prayer of the Spirit, we're more like someone using a waterwheel (an electric pump, today) to obtain a nearly continuous flow of life-giving water out of a deep aquifer. There are times when the Spirit reveals the loving presence of God in such a way that quenches our parched souls with a sense of God's loving presence.

In the fourth type of intimacy, Divine Union, we're more like someone who digs so deep that they suddenly strike an underground river. Pressurized living water erupts like an artesian fountain. The Holy Spirit reveals God's love to us in such intensity that we can barely contain it. Such moments are often once-in-a-lifetime events and are profoundly transforming.

Let me tell you about a couple of mine.

From Presence to Absence

I wanted to study at Wheaton College—a Christian liberal arts school outside Chicago—because they took the intellectual side of faith seriously. However, as someone who grew up with an absent and disengaged father, Wheaton's emphasis on the importance of spiritual experience proved equally transformational. I quickly joined one of the many prayer groups (a very helpful type of "climbing team") dotting the campus community. We celebrated Wheaton's rich history of God breaking into the campus community in seasons of revival and asked God to breathe life into us again. Noting my spiritual hunger, our group leader suggested I read *The Practice of the Presence of God* written by a seventeenth-century monk named Brother Lawrence.

The Practice of the Presence of God

I was deeply moved by Lawrence's goal to remain in intimate contact with God no matter what he was doing throughout the day. He truly believed "there is nothing in the world more sweet and delightful than a life of continual conversation with God."[16] Following Lawrence's direction, I started peppering my life with "prayer pauses"—brief moments throughout the day when I turned my attention to God and invited him into what I was doing at that moment.

Then one night, something remarkable happened—something akin to the "Prayer of Union" described by Teresa of Ávila. One minute I was sitting in one of Wheaton's many prayer chapels. The next I was walking on a garden path beside a vast river. Massive trees towered over me. Fruit of every conceivable (and inconceivable) color, shape, and size burst from their heavy-laden branches. Indescribable fragrances—like a mixture of cinnamon, lavender, and honeysuckle—overwhelmed my senses. A shimmering radiance filled the air.

That's when I realized, *I am not alone.* Someone walked beside me, someone as terrifying and "other" as a wild animal yet gentle and familiar as the breeze on my face. When that someone "spoke," the words registered more in my heart than in my ears. Yet the message was unmistakable: it was an invitation, a beckoning, into a deeper experience of divine love than I had ever dreamed possible.

I don't know if that experience lasted a few seconds or a few hours. I gradually found myself once again sitting alone in that rather ordinary chapel. Overwhelmed with the "nearness" of God's love, I spent the next hour singing God's praises at the top of my lungs. It was one of the most extraordinary things I have ever experienced—and I thought it was the beginning of a season, or maybe even a lifetime, of feeling indescribable intimacy with God.

Only it wasn't.

Over the course of the term, God began to disappear from my life just like my earthly father had in my youth. My sense of God's presence evaporated. My prayer times grew flat. Answers to prayer ceased. A breakup with a girlfriend I thought I would marry nearly crushed me. My best friend took a term off, and I ended up with a random (and deeply troubled) roommate. I struggled with my classes and ended up with the worst GPA of my life. I told my prayer group leader that I wanted to write a new book, *The Practice of the Absence of God.*

The Dark Night of the Soul

It was my English professor, Dr. McClatchey, who offered me the greatest solace. He listened carefully to my story. Then he looked both ways, dropped his voice to a whisper, and shared how the most profound God-encounter of his life led to both great blessing and tremendous opposition in the church he pastored before coming to Wheaton. I was spellbound. By the time we finished our conversation, the dining hall was nearly empty. As we both wiped away tears, he leaned close and said, "You must remember that the dark night of the soul is an important step toward intimacy with God."

"What is a dark night of the soul?" I asked. "It sounds terrible."

"It is," he laughed, "and wonderful too. The phrase comes from a famous medieval poem by John of the Cross [1542–91].[17] He discovered that profound experiences with God often blind us spiritually, at least for a season."

"Why is that?" I challenged.

"John of the Cross said that experiencing God is like walking out of a dark church into bright sunlight. The light is so intense that we experience it as darkness until our spiritual eyes adjust to see God's light and love all around us. God allows this lack of a sense of his presence and provision because he wants us to bond with *him* rather than our experience. The dark night drives us deeper into true intimacy and away from mere experientialism."

I sincerely hoped I was in a dark night of the soul, because I sure felt blinded—or maybe I should say *blindsided*. Dr. McClatchey smiled and added, "This would be a good time for you to read *The Screwtape Letters* by C. S. Lewis."

So, I did. Lewis's fictional letters from a senior demon named Screwtape to a student tempter was a lifeline for me. One night, I found a passage that became a beacon for my darkened soul.

> Be not deceived, Wormwood, our [that is, Satan's] cause is never more in jeopardy than when a human, no longer desiring but still intending to do our Enemy's will, looks round upon a universe in which every trace of Him seems to have vanished, and asks why he has been forsaken, and still obeys.[18]

I determined to keep on obeying, to keep on praying, to keep on meditating, to keep on seeking to practice God's presence, no matter how far away he felt.

My term ended not with a bang but a whimper. Nothing changed in my life. Yet as I walked out of my dorm room for the last time that year, feeling spiritually bloodied and beaten, I recognized that something had changed in me. I didn't have words for it then, but now I know that drawing on the bottled oxygen of my past encounters with him had given me the strength to keep on climbing.

From Absence to Presence

On my way home for break, I went to a party at Penn State to visit with friends I had made on a Cru summer project in Wildwood, New Jersey, the summer before. One of those friends, Sue Jordan, seemed startled to see me there. After she recovered herself a bit, she asked, "Do you think you might have time to get together while you're here?"

When we met the next day, Sue surprised me by pulling out a handwritten letter. She passed it to me and sighed, "I wrote this to you because I thought you might be the only person who might understand what I am going through."

Puzzled, I took the letter as she added, "I never sent it, but when I saw you last night, I knew I had to ask you to read it."

"I would be honored," I whispered. (Somehow it felt like a holy moment.)

Sue took one more deep breath and added, "Before you read it, can I ask you a question?"

"Anything," I replied as I noted her thumbs clenched between her fists.

"Have you ever heard of *the dark night of the soul*?"

My mouth dropped open as I nodded like a slow-motion bob-blehead doll.

"Good," she smiled as she relaxed her shoulders. "Then this will make a lot more sense."

It did. In fact, her letter read like pages stolen from my journal. Her hunger to know God matched mine unlike any climbing partner I had ever known. She knew that experiencing God's love is more like getting a new oxygen tank on an exhausting climb than a mountaintop experience. Long before I realized we were soulmates, I knew she was a great soul.

When we both returned for a second summer in Wildwood, Sue began raiding the library of books on knowing God I had brought for the summer. Many afternoons I returned from work to find her waiting outside my room, completed book in hand. For an entire summer, we sat in the backyard discussing knowing God for hours. Slowly, she began to open up to me about her spiritual journey. Slowly, I opened up to her about mine. By the end of the summer, we were head over heels in love. We married that December. After her Penn State graduation, we moved into a cozy off-campus apartment for my final terms at Wheaton. And "we knew that we knew that we knew" that God is a God of intimacy and answered prayer.

A Climbing Guide for the Disciple's Descent into
INTIMACY

Cultivating **Intimacy** in solitude is no easy task. Yet certain prayer practices can slowly help us develop a more intimate relationship with God. Here are a few that have greatly helped me.

Filling Prayer
Filling prayer is similar to the practice of biblical meditation. We flood our minds with truth about God's love by choosing verses

describing God's love for us and then turning them over and over in our minds. Some good places to start might be:

1. The first words of the disciple's prayer: "Our heavenly *Father*, I make holy your name."
2. The words the Father proclaimed over Jesus at his baptism: "You are my Son, whom I love; with you I am well pleased" (Luke 3:22).
3. One of Jesus's parables concerning God's love, such as the parable of the good father (Matt. 7:9–11), the lost sheep (Luke 15:4–7), the lost coin (Luke 15:8–10), or the prodigal son (Luke 15:11–32).

There are plenty of other verses to explore as well. Sue once made a "Love Journal" in which she wrote out over one hundred biblical passages describing God's love.

After meditating on these words day and night, they will slowly begin to soak into your consciousness and transform your thinking. I can tell Jesus's words have taken root in my soul when it becomes natural for me to sing them. Sometimes I borrow a melody from another song, and sometimes a new tune comes to mind. Over the course of my life, I've developed a vast repertoire of little ditties that work what C. S. Lewis referred to as "deeper magic"[19] in my soul. I rarely share any of them with others (they are not that kind of song), but they help me define my identity as one "beloved of God."

Emptying Prayer

Emptying prayer (sometimes called "Centering Prayer") is the exact opposite of filling prayer. Instead of flooding your mind with thoughts about God, you seek to still your soul by emptying your mind of every reality except the presence of the love of

God within you through the Holy Spirit and/or surrounding you through creation.

Through emptying prayer, we can obey the Lord's command to: "Be still, and know that I am God" (Ps. 46:10). Like the psalmist, we slowly learn to be able to say, "I have stilled and quieted my soul, like a child who just finished nursing is my soul within me" (Ps. 131:2 GDS). It takes some practice to learn how to *not* think and simply *be* present to the Presence of the God of love, but it is well worth it.

Start by sitting still in a "quiet-ish" place with your phone off and in another room. Take a few "cleansing breaths" in through the nose and out through the mouth—like you are about to shoot a foul shot, or any other activity requiring focus. Then simply seek to be aware of God's loving presence around and within you.

Don't worry if your mind wanders. I guarantee it will, probably every seven seconds. That's just the way our brains work. That is where the practice comes in. Each time your mind wanders, you can train your mind to let go of those thoughts so it can wander back into God's presence. I remember reading of one person trying to grow in emptying prayer who told their mentor, "I'm such a failure at this prayer. In twenty minutes, I've had ten thousand thoughts!" Without missing a beat, her mentor replied, "How wonderful! You've had ten thousand opportunities to train your heart to return to God."[20]

Many people find that an excellent way to do this is to find a brief "reminder prayer"—usually just a word or two—to draw the gaze of your soul back to God. I often use the first words of the Lord's Prayer, "Our Father in heaven," or more simply, "Abba Father," or even just, "Abba," to let go of the distracting thought and return to being present with God.

It may or may not make a big difference in those seven minutes, but over time you will find that you have trained your mind to wander to God's loving presence. Slowly it will become easier and easier to believe that your loving heavenly Father is with you at every moment of your day. Then, like Brother Lawrence, you'll be ready to "practice the presence of God" in *everything* you do.

*Scan the QR code below for the backstory on Gary's climb toward **Intimacy**.*

SIX

PRAYER
Defeating the Demogorgon

"If you remain in me and my words remain in you,
ask whatever you wish, and it will be done for you. This is
to my Father's glory, that you bear much fruit,
showing yourselves to be my disciples."

—Jesus of Nazareth (John 15:7–8)

George Mallory and Sandy Irvine's deaths on the 1924 British
Everest expedition did little to blunt the fervor of those longing to reach the "last great goal of mankind." A worldwide Great
Depression did. So it was not until 1933 that the Royal Geographical
Society obtained permission from the thirteenth Dalai Lama to
follow the expedition camp pathway Mallory and company pio-
neered. Months of effort led to the recovery of Sandy Irvine's ice
axe at 27,760 feet, but horrible weather and illness beat back every
attempt at summiting. Everest had once again defeated one of the
greatest climbing teams ever assembled.

That same year, a second and stranger expedition set out from
Britain. Inspired by George Mallory's writings, World War I hero

Maurice Wilson announced his intention to fly his biplane to the Himalayas. His goal? Fly over Mallory's expedition camps, crash-land his plane on Everest's slopes, and *walk* to the summit. Harebrained as it was, Wilson's plan captured the imagination of the British public every bit as much as the Royal Geographical Society's official expedition. One newspaper headline declared his journey the "Most Amazing Air Adventure Ever Attempted."[1]

British officials disagreed. Wilson's unsanctioned trip posed a significant diplomatic embarrassment to the crown. Officials strove to deter him from the moment he first publicized his plans. Just five days before his departure date, the British Air Ministry cabled Wilson: "BE WARNED THAT IN NO CIRCUMSTANCES ARE YOU TO BE PERMITTED TO MAKE THE ATTEMPT."[2] The resistance only energized Wilson. Although he possessed neither the aviation skills nor the mountaineering experience for such a venture, no Everest climber—not even Mallory—ever matched Wilson's confidence. Cheered on by well-wishers, he pointed his biplane toward Everest and launched.

Flying a biplane with maximum range of less than five hundred miles, Wilson had to hopscotch eight thousand miles across Europe, the Middle East, and South Asia. Despite bulletins from the British Air Ministry to stop him at all costs, Wilson's compelling vision and irresistible charm won him friends (and fuel) at airfield after airfield. Wilson made it all the way to India before officials finally resorted to impounding his plane. Undeterred, Wilson hired some of the same Sherpa porters who had just assisted the official 1933 British expedition, disguised himself as a Buddhist priest, and snuck into Tibet to continue his obsessive journey to the summit on foot. He wrote in his journal, "This will be a last effort, and I feel successful."[3]

Unfortunately, convincing the mountain of the inevitability of his success proved significantly more difficult than convincing himself. Even if Wilson had the requisite skills and equipment, he knew nothing of the acclimatization process required for such a journey and carried no oxygen tanks. Altitude sickness soon left him with debilitating fatigue, intellectual disorientation, and a loss of coordination known as "mountain drunkenness." Once this far gone, altitude sickness renders even the most experienced climbers unable to accomplish the simplest of tasks. They simply give up, sit down, and refuse to move. Which is precisely what happened to Wilson.

Still nine thousand vertical feet below the summit, Wilson wrote in his diary, "Off again, gorgeous day . . ." but then never left his tent.[4] It would be his final journal entry. The 1934 British expedition discovered his body in his sleeping bag, curled up in the fetal possession. The strangest climber in Everest history never made it above twenty-two thousand feet. While his official cause of death was listed as "exposure," Maurice Wilson's real killer was *overconfidence*.

This Kind

Overconfidence also forms the theme of one of the strangest recorded teaching sessions in the college of Jesus. The Teacher took Peter, James, and John the Beloved on a three-day prayer retreat atop a nearby mountain, leaving his other nine disciples behind (Luke 9:28). Peter, James, and John clearly got the long end of this stick. They experienced Jesus's transfiguration, heard the voice of God from heaven, and visited with Moses and Elijah. As prayer retreats go, this one was a real winner.

When the four prayer partners rejoined the other disciples, they found them arguing with a large crowd. The man in the center of the fray told Jesus: "Teacher, I brought you my son, who is possessed by a spirit that has robbed him of speech. . . . I asked your disciples to drive out the spirit, but they could not" (Mark 9:17–18).

Jesus's response reveals significant frustration. "You unbelieving generation . . . how long shall I stay with you? How long shall I put up with you?" (v. 19).[5]

Clearly, something about this episode really got under Jesus's skin. It's not the demon. Jesus casts it out with a word. We discover a more likely explanation for Jesus's frustration after he and his disciples find lodging. His chagrined students ask, "Why couldn't we drive it out?"

Jesus replied, "This kind can come out only by prayer and fasting" (v. 29).[6]

This makes the disciple's lack of prayer the most obvious explanation for Jesus's frustration. Like Maurice Wilson, their overconfidence had led them astray. And why not? They have good reason to be overconfident. Jesus had already granted them "power and authority to drive out all demons" (Luke 9:1),[7] and they used this authority effectively. "They drove out many demons and anointed many sick people with oil and healed them" (Mark 6:13). So why not now?

Some scholars propose that their authority over demons on their first preaching tour was only a temporary impartation. Now they had to learn how to seek such authority on their own. Others suspect the issue is that "this kind" of demon required greater authority than the run-of-the-mill demons they had previously encountered. Either way, the solution was a life of prayer (and likely fasting), and this was a practice the nine had obviously failed. And this is likely why Jesus is so piqued. The disciples' overconfidence had led them to completely miss the point of one of the most crucial practices in the curriculum of his college: **Prayer**.

School of Prayer
While prayer was part of all Jewish education, Jesus's overarching commitment to prayer goes far beyond other rabbis of his day. As

noted in the last chapter, a significant portion of the Sermon on the Mount centers on prayer. At least 20 percent of Jesus's parables deal with prayer. Jesus devotes nearly half of his Farewell Discourse (John 13–17) to praying with his students and teaching them about prayer. Luke records no less that nine specific occasions when Jesus prays with his students or models prayer for them.[8]

As I've suggested before, **Prayer** and education are inseparable because education and the knowledge of God are inseparable. When his disciples (finally stripped of their overconfidence) asked their Teacher, "Lord, teach us to pray" (Luke 11:1), Jesus's **Instruction** began with the **Intimacy** of the experiential knowledge of their Father God: "Our Father in heaven." But it doesn't stop there. He invites them to ask for public answers to prayer connected to the kingdom of God.

The next three elements found in the Lord's Prayer—that the Father's name be hallowed, that his kingdom come, and that his will be done on earth as it is heaven—are basically three different ways of asking the same thing.[9] Incredibly, Jesus teaches his disciples (and us) that their prayers are somehow connected to the kingdom of heaven breaking into this present evil age so that the will of God in heaven becomes reality upon the earth.[10] As theologian David Wells asserts:

> What then, is the nature of petitionary prayer? It is, in essence, rebellion—rebellion against the world in its fallenness, the absolute and undying refusal to accept as normal what is pervasively abnormal. . . . Petitionary prayer only flourishes where there is a twofold belief: first, that God's name is hallowed too irregularly, His kingdom has come too little, and His will is done too infrequently; second, that God Himself can change this situation.[11]

Now we begin to see the reason why Jesus was so frustrated with his prayerless students. Somehow, our prayers connect to the invisible battle between the kingdom of God and supernatural forces of evil. Jesus's disciples asking their heavenly Father for his kingdom to come and his will to be done on earth is a crucial part of this battle. God moves in answer to the prayers of his disciples to overcome any demonic opposition to the will of God.[12]

This is not the way most American Christians think about the kingdom of God. We tend to demonize people—even other Christians—because we think our battle is against "flesh and blood" when in reality, our battle is against spiritual and structural forces of evil (Eph. 6:12). Ironically, popular culture often reflects this biblical worldview better than most churches. Think of the breakout Netflix show *Stranger Things*. Scientists in a secret CIA laboratory accidentally open a rift between our world and "the Upside Down"—an alternate dimension that is a dark reflection or "echo" of our world. "It is a place of decay and death. . . . It is right next to you, and you don't even see it."[13]

A "Demogorgon" from the Upside Down finds its way through the rift. It enters our world intent on setting up his headquarters for world domination in Hawkins, Indiana. The Demogorgon captures a mild-mannered student, Will Byers, and drags him into the Upside Down as his captive. The only thing standing between the Demogorgon and Will's demise (not to mention the end of the world) is a band of middle school students. Under the tutelage of El—a telekinetic runaway from the CIA lab—the teenagers learn that their battle is not against their fellow townspeople but the Demogorgon who has taken them captive to his will. They have to learn how to outwit the Demogorgon so El can use her telekinesis to rescue Will.

[Spoiler Alert.] Of course, this being Hollywood (not Indiana), nothing goes exactly as planned. In the end, they have to help El grow strong enough to defeat the Demogorgon, rescue Will from the Upside Down, and save the world. (At least until the next season when they realize the Demogorgon was sent by someone even more powerful.)

Sounds pretty far-fetched, right? That is, until you read what Jesus taught his disciples next: "When a strong man, fully armed, guards his own house, his possessions are safe. But when someone stronger attacks and overpowers him, he takes away the armor in which the man trusted and divides up his plunder" (Luke 11:21–22). It sounds a lot more like El and friends versus a Demogorgon than your typical church prayer group.

That would mean Jesus is frustrated with his non-praying students because they are supposed to be warriors in an invisible battle against the spiritual forces of evil resisting the kingdom of God. Jesus is stronger than "this kind" of demon. Clearly Jesus expects his disciples to become spiritual Els capable of defeating this Demogorgon, I mean "demon." Their participation in the life of prayer (and fasting) Jesus had modeled for them *could* have rescued the boy from the demon afflicting him, but they we were too overconfident in their own abilities to bother to pray.

So how might world-saving prayer work in the modern world?

Silencing the Voice

Most people have heard the amazing story of the rescue of the British troops trapped at Dunkirk in World War II. That's especially true if you've watched the *two* 2018 Academy Award–nominated movies chronicling the amazing events: *Dunkirk*, directed by Christopher Nolan, and *Darkest Hour*, directed by Joe Wright.[14] In May of 1940, Adolf Hitler's blitzkrieg invasion and occupation of Belgium and then France left four hundred thousand British troops trapped on the beach at Dunkirk, France. The twenty-one miles across the English Channel to Britain and safety might as well have been the entire Pacific Ocean. To win World War II, Hitler needed only to order his Panzer tank divisions to move in to capture the helpless soldiers. Without an army to defend their shores, England would almost certainly have fallen to a Nazi invasion more than eighteen months before the United States even entered the war.

Yet Hitler never gave the order. In full view of Hitler's frustrated generals, a massive flotilla of British ships—military boats, fishing boats, sailboats, leisure boats, and yachts—pulled up to the only pier in Dunkirk and rescued nearly all of the four hundred thousand soldiers. Even the *Princess Elizabeth* luxury steamer completed four trips, rescuing 1,673 men. All while Hitler's ground generals did next to nothing because Hitler refused to give the order to attack.

Scholars have proposed countless theories to account for the world-shaping blunder of Hitler's silence. Allow me to propose a theory that never made it into either of the movies—the students and faculty at the Bible College of Wales (BCW) in the United Kingdom. Founder and president of BWC Rees Howells (1879–1950) was known as a man with deep confidence and experience in the power of prayer. When word of the German invasion of Belgium and France reached their campus, Howells called the faculty and student body to prayer from seven to midnight each evening. When news of England's "darkest hour" at Dunkirk arrived, Howells led the faculty and students in day-and-night prayer for nearly a week.

As far as we know, what made the prayers of the BCW community unique among the countless other prayers lifted up by men and women throughout the British empire and beyond was their focus. Rather than targeting their prayers upon the visible war between the British and German armies, Howells looked to the invisible war in the heavens. He held strongly to the apostle Paul's instruction that "Our struggle is not against flesh and blood, but against the rulers, against the authorities, against the powers of this dark world and against the spiritual forces of evil in the heavenly realms" (Eph. 6:12). So, led by God's Spirit, Howells had the BCW community pray against whatever demonic "voice" might be guiding Hitler.[15] And like the middle schoolers in *Stranger Things* battling against the forces of "the Upside Down," they may very well have been correct.

It turns out Hitler did have an occult "voice" guiding him—a voice later confirmed by British diplomat Nevil Henderson[16] and a psychologist who examined Hitler shortly after World War I.[17] The voice had flawlessly guided Hitler's rise to power in Germany, his annexation of Austria, and his rapid victory over Belgium and France. Yet, as nearly as we can tell, as soon as the BCW's students and faculty began to pray for God's help in resisting the "strong man," Hitler's voice went silent. Unsure as to how to function without this supernatural guidance, Hitler hesitated to give the order to attack the British troops at Dunkirk.

Am I claiming the prayers of the students and faculty of the Bible College of Wales were singularly responsible for the defeat of Hitler? Absolutely not. But, given Jesus's teaching, is it really that far-fetched to believe "this kind" of world-ruining spiritual evil can only be driven out by prayer and fasting?

Fruitful Disciples

This invites the question, just how does someone train to become the kind of person whose prayers make a supernatural difference in the world? I mean, there's no secret CIA installation in Hawkins, Indiana, training people to do this, right? Fortunately, Jesus addresses this very issue in a beautiful allegory crafted from the vineyards scattered throughout his students' agrarian society:

"I am the true vine, and my Father is the gardener. . . . You are the branches" (John 15:1, 5).

While his richly textured metaphor presents numerous teaching points, the main gist of his argument is simply this: branches (students) who abide in (dwell in, continue their connection to) the vine (Jesus) will become fruitful. "I am the vine; you are the branches. If you remain in me and I in you, you will bear much fruit" (John 15:5). This fruitfulness is what identifies someone as a true disciple. "This is to my Father's glory, that you bear much fruit, showing yourselves to be my disciples" (John 15:8). As biblical scholar Raymond Brown reminds us, "The sense is not that when the hearers bear fruit, they will become his disciples, but that in bearing fruit they show they are disciples."[18] Jesus provides all the life required for the fruitfulness of his disciples. This life, this grace (John 1:16), this revelation of Jesus and his love (John 14:21), this experiential knowledge of God (John 17:3), works its way deep into the student's life and transforms them into a true disciple.

Jesus weaves nearly every essential in his discipleship curriculum into this one allegory:

> If you remain in me [**Intimacy**] and my words remain in you [**Instruction**], ask whatever you wish [**Prayer**], and it will be done for you. . . . You did not choose me, but I chose you [**Community**] and appointed you so that you might go and bear fruit—fruit that will last [**Embodiment**]—so that whatever you ask in my name [**Prayer**] the Father will give you [**Intimacy**]. This is my command [**Instruction**]: **Love each other.** (John 15:7, 16–17)

This "inside out" approach to growth is radically differently from the Christian moralism ordering men and women to obey God's commands in their own strength. In fact, Jesus specifically warns his disciples that apart from the life he provides, "you can do nothing" (John 15:5). Or, to switch back to our Everest analogy, climbers who abide in (stay connected to) their lifegiving oxygen mask are able to bear the fruit of climbing to the summit.

What's interesting for our discussion here is that the same acclimatization and oxygen tank strategies that help the disciple become like Jesus also enable them to pray like Jesus. Following Jesus's teachings, especially his command to love, transforms us into the kind of people he can entrust with powerful answers to prayer for extending his kingdom "on earth as it is in heaven" (Matt. 6:10). Eugene Peterson translates these prayer verses in this way: "if you make yourselves at home with me and my words are at home in you, you can be sure that whatever you ask will be listened to and acted upon. . . . As fruit bearers, whatever you ask the Father in relation to me, he gives you" (John 15:7, 16 *The Message*).[19] As New Testament scholar Craig Keener asserts, abiding in Jesus and allowing his words to abide in us entails "continuing to love and trust in Jesus, with the assurance that the lover of Jesus, whose **Desires** are ultimately for Jesus's agenda, will receive answered prayer."[20]

A Climbing Guide for the Disciple's Descent into
PRAYER

Of course, **Prayer** is much easier to talk about than to do. That's why so many prayer meetings wind up spending more time "sharing" prayer requests than actually praying. Here are two practices that have helped me.

Petitionary Prayer

Petitionary prayer (sometimes called *intercessory* prayer) is simply asking God to intervene in the world. However, as David Wells asserts, petitionary prayer flourishes when we open our hearts to be broken by the situations in which God's will is not done on earth and open our mouths to act upon his promise that our prayers make a difference in the world. True petitionary prayer is not so much the ordinary prayer every human being (even atheists) prays when they face a personal need. It is prayer offered on behalf of others' needs, especially for our neighbors and even enemies.

1. Begin praying daily for one problem in the world, or just in a single person's life, that requires divine intervention: a "this kind" that can only come out with prayer. It could be a neighbor facing cancer, a friend on drugs, the houseless people in your city, or *any place* where God's will in the heavens needs to *come* upon the earth.

2. Don't stop praying. Allow the prayers to change you. If you've roped yourself to a climbing partner, pray together and hold one another accountable to continue praying. Jesus taught his students that agreeing together in prayer upon the earth is often a prerequisite for an answer from heaven (Matt. 18:19).

3. Don't lose heart. Jesus told his disciples in one of his most powerful prayer parables, the parable of the persistent widow, "to show them that they should always pray and not give up" (Luke 18:1). He never explains why answered prayer often requires persistent "knocking, asking, and seeking," but it is a consistent theme in his prayer parables (Luke 11:5–13).

4. Don't be surprised by setbacks. Just like Jesus's first disciples, the biographies of every effective prayer warrior I have ever studied are filled with their struggles with unanswered prayer. Sometimes God reveals why a prayer goes unanswered (2 Cor. 12:7–10), but that is usually not the case. Learning to trust God with this mystery while continuing to advance in our practice of prayer is a sign of a true world healer.

5. Remember, prayer is a relationship. Like all relationships, prayer involves communication and collaboration. We cannot

allow prayer to become a means of our trying to talk God into something. As Richard Foster reminds us, "Real prayer comes not from gritting our teeth but from falling in love."[21]

Fasting

Fasting is a practice designed to remedy the universal human complaint: "I don't have time to pray." By voluntarily giving up an activity, we free up time in our busy schedules to pray. For instance, people are amazed how much time they have for prayer when they turn off their phone for certain hours of the day. Freed from the distraction of our phone's constant cry for attention (a.k.a. "notifications"), we are able to focus our prayers as never before.

The same can be accomplished by giving up the activity of preparing, eating, and cleaning up meals. Often the only way climbing partners can find time in their busy schedules to meet together to pray is by giving up a meal time to do it. Jesus took Peter, James, and John on a three-day prayer retreat during which they likely fasted. It's doubtful we will ever have Moses and Elijah join our prayer group, but it can be a powerful community practice.[22]

Wheaton in Watts

Sue and I experienced the power of combining petitionary prayer with fasting shortly after we were married. We were selected to lead the small group leader training for Wheaton in Watts—a spring break service-learning trip that originated with the Rev. Dr. E. V. Hill's invitation to Wheaton students to visit his church in South Central Los Angeles to learn how to transform a city neighborhood for good. Forty Wheaton students responded to Dr. Hill's invitation. But as Sue and I sat in the basement lounge of Evans Hall with the ten students who had been chosen to serve with us as small group leaders for the trip, we found ourselves spending more time dealing with everyone's anxiety than training. The idea of going to South Central Los Angeles seemed a lot more romantic when we signed up.

Finally, Henry suggested, "If we are going to Watts, then I think we should pray."

"That's a great idea," I agreed as everyone nodded.

"If we're going to pray, then we should fast!" John piped up.

"That's an idea," I winced. (I like to eat.)

"If we're going to fast, then we should fast for a week," Mimi exclaimed.

"That's a *bad* idea," I countered. (Did I mention how much I like to eat?) But I was quickly outvoted. Many of these student leaders had grown up in traditions where fasting is a normal part of petitionary prayer. They brought Scripture references and handouts from their pastors to the next meeting. One week later, we began our fast.[23]

The plan was simple. Everyone would decide for themselves what they would fast *from*. Most did a water-only fast. Some did juice fasts. At least one prediabetic student simplified their diet for the week under the direction of their doctor. We also decided together what we were fasting *to*. Since our purpose was to pray together, we decided to meet in the basement of Evans Hall from five to seven every night that week. Freed from the time we would have spent eating, everyone would have time in their schedule.

Things were kind of rough at first. Our prayer meetings felt very low energy as our bodies switched over to burning ketones instead of carbs. (This was before anyone knew anything about keto diets.) But as our bodies began to adjust, our prayer times became more and more intense. The sense of God's presence in the room seemed more and more tangible. I arrived late one evening and felt like I hit a wall of spiritual air pressure when I came into the room. I joked with Sue, "The presence of God felt so tangible and 'solid,' that I felt like I could cut out a chunk and put it in my backpack."

After a week of the most remarkable prayer meetings I've ever experienced, we broke our fast with deep-dish pizza (a very bad idea) and prepared for our trip to Los Angeles. We didn't know what God was up to, but we knew it was something special.

"You are here to learn how to minister to a community," Dr. Hill told us in his rich baritone voice. "All of South Central Los Angeles is our parish, not just Watts. Mt. Zion Missionary Baptist's goal is to go block by block, house by house, into the highways and byways of South Central to compel people to come to the wedding feast of the kingdom of God. Each day we will pair you with a team of Mt. Zion's most experienced leaders, who will take you door to door throughout our neighborhoods."

We were there to learn, but that didn't stop us from bringing a "White savior" mentality into the week. It lasted less than twenty-four hours. By the end of our first day (Sunday), we were completely overwhelmed. With a few exceptions, our group of "Wheaties" was nearly entirely White. Only one of us had ever experienced a sabbath bookended by two highly expressive three-hour worship services (Dr. Hill looked at stiff responses and dubbed us "the frozen chosen"). And only one of us had every lived in a Black neighborhood. Like the rest of the group, Sue and I spent the week living with a widow from the church. This was part of Rev. Hill's genius: our fees provided income for the most economically at-risk members of his community, and they provided visiting teams with lodging in their homes. Our host, Etoy, was the warmest, most Christ-filled person we had ever met. She cooked us eggs from her chickens each morning and made us turkey wings for our lunches.

Our conversations with Etoy opened our eyes to an entirely new world as Rev. Hill continued to give our group hours of his time. His often-spontaneous lectures instructed us on the history of South Central, the Watts riots, and the injustices suffered by the African American community. He patiently but relentlessly peeled back the layers of our racism and privilege better than a graduate degree in sociology. Somehow the prayer and fasting for the week had broken open our hearts to receive his words of the kingdom. He transformed our vision of the kingdom in a manner that transformed Sue and me for life.

Our neighborhood sessions accompanying teams of church members proved to be the laboratory to support Dr. Hill's lectures. They went surprisingly well. Nearly every one of our groups experienced someone coming to faith in Christ—sometimes in dramatic fashion. One day, the Mt. Zion trainers for Sue's and my neighborhood group, Dorothy and Arthur, knocked on a screen door as Dorothy called out, "Anyone here want to talk about Jesus?"

A woman inside called back, "We need Jesus! Get on in here."

When we entered, it was obvious she had been crying. Her children as well. Dorothy and our church coleader began by helping the woman solve a family conflict with her teenage son. Then they provided church resources to help the woman pay her electric bill. Only then did Dorothy finally bring up "the gospel." Two hours later, we left a woman "filled with joy because [she] had come to believe in God—[she] and [her] whole household" (Acts 16:34).

Sue and I and our Wheaton teammates didn't play much of a role. Still, it was breathtaking to watch. As we walked back to the church building, I said to Arthur, "That was amazing! No wonder you want to do this ministry when things like this happen every day."

Arthur arched his brow and replied, "They *don't* normally go this well. We take teams of White folk and Black folk through these neighborhoods every week, and we have never seen a community response like this. Just this morning, we were all asking, 'What is going on this week?' We decided that nothing changed for us, so it must be your group."

He stopped and motioned to me with his fingers cupped like a fighter inviting a punch. "Okay, spill it. What is going on with you all?"

"I don't know," I replied, shoving my hands in my pockets. "We did put a lot of prayer into this."

"How much prayer?" he asked.

I didn't want to sound all braggy, but he deserved an explanation. "Well, twelve of us did fast and pray for a week."

"A week!" Arthur pursed his lips and nodded. "That explains it."

By then we were just walking into the church parking lot. Arthur called out to Dorothy and other Mt. Zion leaders waiting outside, "I figured it out!" he proclaimed proudly, "These kids are prayer warriors."

"I knew it! I knew it!" Dorothy called back. "Thank you, Jesus."

I could not agree more. "Thank you, Jesus!" Mt. Zion taught us more than we could have ever imagined possible about ministering to a community. But our Teacher wanted us to learn something about the power of **Prayer** (and fasting) as well.

Prayer is integral to experiencing intimacy with God, but it is also integral to our colaboring with Jesus in extending the kingdom and the will of God on earth as it is in heaven. Students who claim to follow Jesus and his teachings but refuse to enter into the difficult but rewarding process of learning to pray are only kidding themselves. They are spiritual Maurice Wilsons whose overconfidence in their own abilities vexes their Teacher every bit as much as the nine disciples who could not help a boy with "this kind" of demon. He wants to form us into the kind of people he can entrust with answers to prayer that make Demogorgons tremble. Disciples who abide in Jesus and his teachings, especially his command to love, and therefore bear the fruit of the kingdom. Our *descent* into a deeper and deeper experience of the love of God imparts the transforming life of Jesus into the disciple who, if they will only remain in Jesus, will bear the fruit of prayerfully participating in God's kingdom coming on earth as it is in heaven.

*Scan the QR code below for the backstory on Gary's climb toward **Prayer**.*

SEVEN

LOVE

"A new command I give you: Love one another. As I have loved you, so you must love one another. By this everyone will know that you are my disciples, if you love one another."

—Jesus of Nazareth (John 13:34–35)

While the mythical Yeti haunts Himalayan folklore, the true invisible men of Everest climbing come from a tiny ethnic group known as the Sherpa. One can read countless stories from Everest climbers without a single mention of the Sherpa. Yet summiting Everest would be virtually impossible without them. Thousands of years of living at high altitudes has granted the Sherpa thirty genetic adaptations enabling them to thrive. Rather than requiring a gradual buildup of red blood cells through short-term acclimatization, Sherpa DNA directs their bodies to use the available oxygen in high altitudes more efficiently. This permanent genetic acclimatization allows the Sherpa to flourish where foreigners achieving short-term acclimatization often falter. In other words, life at high altitude didn't just transform the Sherpas as individuals but as a *people*.

This fact led to one of the most remarkable coincidences in exploration history: the first Westerners to arrive in the Himalayas seeking to summit Everest were greeted by perhaps the only people on earth who could help them accomplish the feat. The first British explorer to recognize the Sherpa's unique ability to function at high altitude was the team doctor for the 1921 British expedition, Dr. Alexander Kellas. Kellas lived among the Sherpa for years and became the first Westerner to seriously study altitude sickness and the use of bottled oxygen in climbing. In a strange reversal, Kellas (and later Mallory) taught the Sherpa how to climb mountains. For centuries, the Sherpa considered the peaks surrounding them too holy to approach. Kellas befriended the Sherpa and worked with them to summit ten Himalayan peaks together.

Tragically, Dr. Kellas died from a heart attack early in the first British Everest expedition (1921). Without his intercession, future teams regarded the Sherpa as little more than ready-made porters for carrying their bulky supplies. The Sherpa were glad to assist their well-paying employers on the first twelve Everest foreign expeditions. Still, they wondered why no one considered consulting them as partners in the endeavor. So it should be no surprise that after three decades of climbing, foreign expeditions to Everest failed to summit even once.[1]

All that changed in 1952. Sherpa Tenzing Norgay led a Swiss expedition within eight hundred vertical feet of the summit. The climbing leader for the upcoming 1953 British expedition, New Zealander Edmund Hillary, immediately took notice. He invited Tenzing to join the British expedition as his climbing partner. From that day forward, Sherpa have guided nearly every Everest expedition. The Sherpa became the true heroes of Everest climbing—the right people, in the right place, at the right time to help the world achieve the impossible.

Just like Jesus's disciple John the Beloved.

The Room Where It Happens

If I were to designate walk-up music for John the Beloved, I would choose "The Room Where It Happens" from Lin-Manuel Miranda's Tony Award–winning musical *Hamilton*. The song—brilliantly performed by Leslie Odom Jr.—portrays Aaron Burr's complaint that Treasury Secretary Alexander Hamilton made our fledgling nation's most important political decisions behind closed doors. No one else was in "the room where it happens."

However, Burr's complaint wasn't so much that Hamilton made these decisions secretly. He was more concerned about who was being left out of the decision-making process (him!). By the time the song ends, Burr reaches a conclusion that will shape the rest of his life (and Alexander Hamilton's as well): "I've gotta be in the room! Click-boom! The room where it happens."[2]

John the Beloved

The disciple known as John the Beloved seems to have come to the same conclusion as Aaron Burr. Rather than playing second fiddle to his older brother, James—as would be expected of a second-born son in his day—John made sure he was in the "room where it happens" for nearly every significant event in the college of Jesus. As mentioned in Chapter One (**Desire**), John the Beloved was in the room where it happened when John the Baptist gave his first two students a chance to interview for the college of Jesus (John 1:35–39). He was on the beach where it happened when Jesus performed a miraculous catch of fish and called his first students to become fishers of people (Luke 5:1–11; Matt. 4:21–22; Mark 1:19–20). He was at the wedding where it happened when

Jesus performed his first miracle by changing water into wine (John 2:1–12). John was in the synagogue where it happened when Jesus cast out his first demon (Mark 1:29–39). He was also one of only three students in the room where it happened when Jesus raised a little girl from the dead (Mark 5:35–43). As mentioned in Chapter Six (**Prayer**), John was one of only three students who witnessed the transfiguration on the mountain where it happened (Luke 9:28–36; Matt. 17:1–9; Mark 9:1–9). He was one of only two students sent to arrange for the room where the Last Supper happened (Luke 22:7–13).[3]

A Much-Needed Transformation

But, before we cheer too loud for John the Beloved, we have to contend with the reality that, just like Aaron Burr, his longing to be in the room where it happens reveals a much darker story. John doesn't start out as precisely the kind of student most teachers would choose for admission to a school founded upon the priority of loving others. When James and John witness someone casting out demons in Jesus's name, they ignore Jesus's teaching on including others and instead inform their Teacher, "We told him to stop, because he was not one of us" (Mark 9:38). When a Samaritan village refuses hospitality to their traveling college, James and John ignore Jesus's teaching on turning the other cheek and instead ask Jesus, "Lord, do you want us to call fire down from heaven to destroy them?" (Luke 9:51–56). No wonder Jesus nicknamed the brothers "the sons of thunder" (Mark 3:13–18).

Worst of all, James and John seem to be at the center of the disciples' running debate over "who is the greatest among them."[4] Almost every time Jesus instructed his students concerning his forthcoming death, the cost of following him, or the importance of being like a child, his students responded by campaigning for spiritual valedictorian. Finally, James and John shamelessly recruit their own *mother* to pressure Jesus into naming them co-vice presidents of the kingdom of God. One day, she knelt before Jesus and asked for "a favor."

"First, tell me what you want," Jesus responded warily.

She replied, "Grant that one of my sons may sit at your right and the other at your left when you become king" (Matt. 20:20–21 GDS).[5]

Like Aaron Burr, the sons of thunder were angling for *permanent* appointments in the room where it happens—shamelessly leveraging their mother to try to *make* it happen.

Of course, Jesus refused their request; only now he had a bigger problem. When his other students heard about James and John's request, they became indignant with the brothers. (Possibly because they didn't think of it first.) A private rebuke of James and John's selfish ambition wouldn't be enough. So Jesus called together his angry students and offered some choice **Instruction**:

> You know that the rulers of the Gentiles lord it over
> them, and their high officials exercise authority over
> them. Not so with you. Instead, whoever wants to
> become great among you must be your servant, and
> whoever wants to be first must be your slave—just as the
> Son of Man did not come to be served, but to serve, and
> to give his life as a ransom for many. (Matt. 20:25–28)

How these words must have shocked Jesus's students. A *servant* in Jesus's day was the lowest of professions. They performed the most menial of household tasks. A *slave* was lower still. Normally a prisoner of war or an indentured servant who may have sold themselves into slavery for social advancement (at tremendous cost), a slave's money, time, and future were all, strictly speaking, at the disposal of their master.

But there was no mistake: Jesus selected his words very carefully. He needed his students to know that while the authoritarian leaders (Romans) used the power of their position to meet their own needs, the servant leaders of the kingdom of God were to use their power only to meet the needs of others. The more needs they met, the better servant leader they became. Just as Jesus would do everything in his power to give his life for the world, he wanted his students to know that true kingdom greatness dwells not in positions, accomplishments, or even being in the room where it happens. It flows only from a heart of other-centered **Love**.

Beloved

The beautiful part of this story is that John the Beloved took Jesus's teaching to heart. As I mentioned earlier, it is impossible to perfectly align Matthew and Mark's chronology with John's Gospel. Still, it seems likely that Jesus's rebuke of James and John's request for positions of power takes place late in Jesus's ministry. If so, it helps explain a remarkable shift in John the Beloved's character. Beginning in chapter 13 of his Gospel—the night of Jesus's Last Supper with his disciples—*love* moves from a minor subject to the dominant theme. What better accounts for this dramatic change in John the Beloved than Jesus catching him (and James and their mom) red-handed in their selfish ambition?[6]

All of Jesus's students were in the room where Jesus celebrated their final meal together, yet only John seemed to have been paying full attention. John alone begins his account of Jesus's Last Supper with the summary: Jesus "had loved his disciples during his ministry on earth, and now he showed them the full extent of his love" (John 13:1 GDS). John alone tells us how Jesus began their evening by washing his students' feet like a household servant (John 13:4–15). John alone records how Jesus concludes the first part of their evening together by equating loving service with genuine discipleship. "A new command I give you: Love one another. As I have loved you, so you must love one another. By this everyone will know that you are my disciples, if you love one another" (John 13:34–35). As James K. A. Smith asserts, "To follow Jesus is to become a student of the Rabbi who teaches us how to love."[7]

John the Beloved seems to have finally gotten the point of Jesus's kingdom vision. He alone notes the unique nature of Jesus's final prayer requests for his students (John 17:1–26). Jesus asks his Father to help his students (and all his students' students after them) to love one another in such perfect unity that the only possible explanation will be that his love has changed them. "[May they] be brought to complete unity. Then the world will know that you sent me and have loved them even as you have loved me" (John 17:23).

This is how the world will know we follow Jesus, by the unity of our love for one another. This is how everyone will know we are his disciples, by our sacrificial love for the world. Like the Sherpa whose lives at altitude transformed them into a climbing community unlike any on Earth, Jesus expects his discipleship community to demonstrate such profound and permanent acclimatization to the thin air of other-centered love that our love bears witness to the world.

The Beloved Community

John's portrayal of Jesus's life helped the earliest Christians live out these teachings to a remarkable degree. Jesus laid down his life for the world, and Jesus's earliest disciples laid down their lives as well. Acts tells us how the Twelve apostles established a community where "No one claimed that any of their possessions was their own, but they shared everything they had." So much so that "there were no needy persons among them" (Acts 4:32, 34). This mindset continued long after the Twelve had died. Tertullian (160–ca. 225 CE) reported how Roman citizens exclaimed, "Look, how [the followers of Jesus] love one another, and how they are ready to die for each other."[8] They won hearts not so much by brilliantly *preaching* the gospel so much as by authentically *living* the gospel of other-centered love Jesus had modeled for them.

When Trajan Decius (Roman emperor, 249–51 CE) tried to blame an outbreak of the plague on Christians, few believed him. Why? Because Roman citizens knew that Jesus followers were the only people willing to care for those sick from the plague. Christians even ensured plague victims had proper burials if they died. The deeds of the Jesus followers were "on everyone's lips, and they glorified the God of the Christians."[9] Emperor Julian (331–63 CE) attempted to exterminate Jesus's followers throughout the empire, and failed for the same reason Decius did—the other-centered love of Jesus's followers throughout the empire. He later complained, "The godless Galileans [his derisive name for followers of Jesus] support not only their poor, but ours as well." In less than three hundred years, Christianity grew from a small band of frightened disciples to the dominant faith of an empire, not by violence or coercion (that came later), but by their love for one another and acts of service for their neighbors.

I can only pray there will come a day when this is true of followers of Jesus in America as well. As Dr. Martin Luther King Jr. expressed so eloquently:

> Our goal is to create a beloved community and this will require a qualitative change in our souls as well as a quantitative change in our lives.[10]

> The type of love that I stress here is not *eros*, a sort of esthetic or romantic love; not *philia*, a sort of reciprocal love between personal friends; but it is *agape* which is understanding goodwill for all men. It is an overflowing love which seeks nothing in return. It is the love of God

working in the lives of men. This is the love that may
well be the salvation of our civilization.[11]

This is where the disciple's upward/downward journey most closely
approximates that of Everest climbers. Summiting Everest requires
climbers to work in a *low-oxygen* environment. Summiting
discipleship requires disciples to work in a *low–self-interest* environment. This is why following Jesus to the summit of genuine
discipleship is so challenging: because learning to love others as
we love ourselves comes so unnaturally to us. Love is the mark of
authentic discipleship because true other-centered love is the one
characteristic of following Jesus that humans can't counterfeit.

Many students fool themselves into thinking they are genuine
disciples until other-centered love begins to cost them something.
It is easy to love others when they are your friends, family, or
"tribe." But what about loving your enemies, the poor, the widow,
the orphan, the imprisoned, the sick, or *anyone* who cannot pay
you back? Robert Chao Romero reminds us, "As we walk with
Jesus, he sends us to where he has already been at work—among
the poor, the suffering, the immigrant, and all who are cast aside."[12]
This is the true spiritual death zone because genuine love demands
death to our habit of making every decision based upon how it
benefits "me and mine." Instead of preaching exclusive Christian
tribalism, Jesus taught his students:

> There is a saying, "Love your friends and hate your ene-
> mies." But I say: Love your enemies! Pray for the good
> of those who persecute you! In that way you will be
> acting as true children of your Father in heaven, who
> blesses both the evil and the good with sunlight, the just
> and the unjust with rain. If you love only those who love
> you, how is that anything special? Even charlatans do
> that much. If you are friendly only to your friends, how

are you different from everyone else? Even narcissists do that. No, as you follow me you are going to learn to perfectly bless everyone, even as your heavenly Father perfectly blesses all. (Matt. 5:43–48 GDS)

Because He First Loved Us

Don't worry. Jesus does not expect us to grow into the kind of person who can live a life of other-centered love in our own strength. We must follow Jesus on the downward journey into a deeper and deeper experience of the love and life of God. Only there can we find the spiritual oxygen required to make such an arduous climb. John alone records that Jesus taught his students, "As the Father has loved me, so have I loved you. Now remain in my love" (John 15:9). Looking back on Jesus's life and teachings, John the Beloved later writes: "The person who refuses to love doesn't know God at all, because God is love. . . . *We love because he first loved us*" (1 John 4:8, 19 GDS—italics added). The disciple's descent into a deeper and deeper experience of God's love yields a bumper crop of other-centered love for God and the world.

No wonder John begins to describe himself exclusively as "the disciple whom Jesus loved."[13] I doubt it's because John thought Jesus loved him more than the other disciples. I suspect it grows from his finally realizing that his primary identity rested not in any position, power, or accomplishment but in the fact that Jesus loved him. And so can we.

Near the end of his life, former Yale professor and prolific spiritual writer Henri Nouwen answered the question, "Who am I?" with this same simple truth:

I am the beloved. That's the voice Jesus heard when he came out of the Jordan River: "You are my beloved; on you my favor rests." And Jesus says to you and to me that we are loved as he is loved. That same voice is there for you. When you are not claiming that voice, you cannot walk freely in this world.[14]

The love of God experienced in the depth of our being becomes the source of the love of God expressed in our life. Like a mountain climber whose acclimatization journey and cached oxygen tanks enable them to become the kind of person who can climb the world's tallest mountain, the experience of God's love transforms us into the kind of people who can keep Jesus's greatest commandment—to love God with all our heart, soul, mind, and strength, and love our neighbor as ourselves. Just as Jesus's love transformed John's very identity into that of "John the Beloved," our journey to the expedition camp of **Love** shapes and transforms our identity as well. As Psychologist David Benner reminds us, "Our primary vocation [is] to receive love and then let it flow through us. . . . [T]his is not simply my calling. It is also my identity. I am the love that flows through me."[15]

This is the transforming truth, the spiritual oxygen of genuine discipleship: "We love because he first loved us" (1 John 4:19). As John the Beloved later taught his disciples, "This is love: not that we loved God, but that he loved us and sent his Son as an atoning sacrifice for our sins. Dear friends, since God so loved us, we also ought to love one another" (1 John 4:10–11). We give our lives away in other-centered service not to earn God's love but because Jesus has revealed to us the love of the Father by giving away his life for us. "And so we *know* and rely on the love God has for us. *God is love.* Whoever lives in love lives in God, and God in them" (1 John 4:16—italics mine). This is Jesus's goal for us. This is the fruit that demonstrates we are truly his disciples in *any* room where it happens.

The Violence of Love

Few disciples in history have experienced a John the Beloved–like conversion from self-centeredness to other-centered **Love** as dramatically as Oscar Romero (1917–80). Born in a tiny village in the coffee-growing region of northeastern El Salvador, Romero grew up a rule-following, "bookish type."[16] While his father trained him in carpentry, he longed for a life of study. Entering the priesthood afforded him that opportunity. However, before he could finish his doctorate in Rome, El Salvador's acute pastoral shortage prompted church leaders to call him home to serve as a parish priest in an insignificant barrio in the capital city of San Salvador.[17]

Romero seized the opportunity. He rose quickly through the ranks of church leadership by never rocking the boat or causing problems for his superiors. His pastoral colleagues, on the other hand, saw him as a "little inquisitor," a "power freak," and a "wolf in sheep's clothing."[18] What galled them most was Romero's refusal to address the nation's appalling economic and political conditions. El Salvador was one of the poorest countries in Latin America, run by a series of corrupt right-wing governments supported by an oligarchy of fourteen wealthy families who owned more than half the nation's land. Rather than speaking out against injustice, Romero buddied up to the rich and maintained a close relationship with El Salvador's corrupt presidents.[19]

Romero was rewarded for his silence when the nation's elites urged the Vatican to appoint him archbishop of San Salvador, "effectively responsible for shepherding the Catholic Church in all of El Salvador."[20] They knew Romero's self-promoting nature would cause him to "keep clear of the ticking time bomb that was the El Salvadorian economics and politics."[21] Suddenly, Romero was "in the room where it happens," possessing more power than he ever dreamed possible.

But what happened next defied everyone's expectations.

Conversion

Two days before Romero took up his new role, widespread voter fraud and poll intimidation led to the oligarchs' right-wing candidate being named El Salvador's new president. Protests spread throughout the country and continued for weeks. Death squads launched a murderous offensive against protestors, human rights activists, and suspected left-wing rebels, killing thousands. They also harassed, arrested, and even tortured any priest who gave the protestors encouragement or sanctuary. One of the most outspoken of these priests, Rutilio Grande, was a good friend of Oscar Romero. Landowners saw Grande's advocacy for marginalized farm workers as a threat. They arranged for the police to use the unrest as cover to gun down Grande.[22]

Dutiful and silent, as expected, Romero traveled to the rural church where congregants were preparing Grande's body for burial. The soon-to-be Archbishop "spent that day praying and listening to stories of violence and exploitation from the peasants whom Grande had served and stories of his care for them."[23] No one can account for what happened that day, but by the time Romero returned to San Salvador, he was a different person. The power-hungry friend to the rich was gone, replaced by an apostle of "violent love" devoted to justice for the poor.[24] He later explained:

> In all of human history no one has ever encountered a love that was so—how to say it?—so crazy, so exaggerated: giving to the point of being crucified on a cross . . . We have never preached violence, except the violence of the love that led Christ to be nailed to a cross. We preach only the violence that we must each do to ourselves to overcome selfishness and to eliminate *the cruel inequalities among us*. This is not the violence of the sword or the violence of hatred. It is the *violence of love*.[25]

Three Years of Love

Once back in San Salvador, Romero called together the city's priests for their first official meeting under his leadership. They were stunned by his new purpose and demeanor, and that he honestly sought their counsel for what the church should do next. By the end of the day, they agreed that as a prophetic action, they would cancel their parish worship services throughout the city and gather for a single outdoor mass in honor of Grande. Despite opposition from the president, the elite families, and the Vatican ambassador, all sixty-three pastors and chaplains present voted their support.[26]

That Sunday a crowd of more than one hundred thousand worshippers crammed into the city square, with at least two times that many listening on the radio.[27] Romero's homily praised Rutilio Grande for his work for the poor and against corruption and injustice, reminding listeners that justice is merely love of neighbor written large enough to embrace all society. He then exhorted his new flock to continue Grande's work and vowed to do the same himself.

Speaking of Grande's assassination, Romero boldly declared, "How can Christians do such things to each other?" then answered his own question:

> Christ tells us that the sign of the Christian is living the
> new commandment he gives us. It is a commandment
> that tonight becomes fresh in our memory and our
> lives: "As I have loved you, so you also should love one
> another" (John 13:34). . . . Let us not tire of preaching
> love; it is the force that will overcome the world. Let us
> not tire of preaching love. Though we see that waves of
> violence succeed in drowning the fire of Christian love,
> love must win out; it is the only thing that can.[28]

Rejecting the violence perpetrated by both the left and the right, Romero was denounced by the wealthy, vilified in the press, harassed by right-wing government security forces, and threatened by leftist guerrillas. Romero's transformation from a privileged church bureaucrat to a prophetic justice reformer led to one of the most remarkable three-year ministries of **Love** since Jesus. And like Jesus, Romero's ministry ended in martyrdom. One fateful Sunday morning, a right-wing death squad burst into his church and assassinated Romero while he held the bread symbolizing the death of Jesus. Soon his blood mingled with the wine poured to commemorate the blood Jesus shed for the salvation of the world.

Against all odds, the once self-centered Romero approached the summit of discipleship—loving God and serving his nation with other-centered **Love** and with an other-centered death. In the half-century since his assassination, his life and homilies still serve as a spiritual Sherpa, guiding other Jesus followers throughout Latin America on their climb. As Gustavo Gutiérrez declared: "I think that we could say, without exaggeration, that the life and death of Monseñor Romero divides the recent history of the Latin American church into a before and after."[29]

A Climbing Guide for the Disciple's Descent into
LOVE

Learning to give your life away in other-centered service usually requires many trips up and down the mountain of discipleship over many years. Yet, like Oscar Romero, it is a journey we can begin right away. Here are two practices that have helped me on my climb.

Secret Service

From the very beginning of his ministry, Jesus instructed his disciples to give and serve in secret (Matt. 6:1–18). It is an excellent practice for training our hearts to serve out of love for others, not for something we get in return.

1. Prayerfully choose someone in your life to bless. It is okay to start with a friend, but Jesus warns us that blessing a friend who can repay us isn't much of a discipleship challenge (Luke 6:32–36). Serving our enemies is the mark of a true child of our heavenly father (Matt. 5:38–48).
2. Start praying for this person regularly, asking God for wisdom for something you can do to bless them in secret.
3. Serve them in some way they cannot easily trace back to you. It could be slipping them a gift card, writing an encouraging note, paying a bill for them, or cleaning their room. Be creative. Your ego will hate not getting credit, but your soul will grow strong.
4. Keep serving them and others secretly. Give others money, time, or talent without hope of personal return.

Once your spiritual muscles for serving in secret have grown strong, you can begin to learn to secretly serve those outside your normal circle of relationship. Find a need in your neighborhood or an injustice in your community and work to rectify it without calling attention to yourself. There is no limit to what God can accomplish through someone who doesn't care who gets the credit.

Lectio Alius

Context determines everything, especially when it comes to reading a biblical text. If we only read Jesus's teachings in our everyday context, it is all too easy for our eyes to roll over the words and notice only those things our eyes have already seen before.

Lectio Alius—Latin for "another reading"—is a practice designed to help us see around the corner of our own scriptural presuppositions by reading the teachings of Jesus with people of another experience than our own. You can accomplish this in two different ways.

Lectio Alius in solitude: Pick one of Jesus's teaching passages and pray, "Jesus, help me sit at your feet and listen to everything you teach." Then, before you begin reading, imagine you invited someone from a different life experience than your own to read the text with you. In your mind's eye, picture someone of a different age, nationality, socioeconomic status, gender, etc. It could be helpful to put an empty chair in front of you and imagine the person sitting in it. As you read the text, listen for what Jesus might say to you about how the other person might hear "another reading" of the text.

For instance, you might read through the beginning of the Sermon on the Mount with your friend Sam in mind. As you get to each of Jesus's instructions, ask yourself how well you follow it in light of Sam. "Have I judged Sam? Have I been angry with Sam? Have I called him a fool? Have I practiced righteousness just to be noticed by Sam?" You get the idea.

Lectio Alius becomes more powerful the more "otherness" stands between you and the person. For instance, I never truly "saw" the shame and horror of Jesus's sufferings until I read them in the light of James Cone's *The Cross and the Lynching Tree*.[30] Why? Because as a White man, I had never considered the similarity between lynching and crucifixion. Also, I never noticed how first-century Roman soldiers were more like modern police officers than military officers until I read Paul through eyes of Esau McCauley's *Reading While Black*.[31] Suddenly a biblical "theology of policing" opened up to me that I had never noticed before.

Lectio Alius in community: An even more transforming approach occurs when you don't merely *imagine* the other person but instead invite someone from another country, ethnicity, social situation, or economic status to read the teachings of Jesus with you. Suddenly, you will find brand new applications popping out of the text. Or, better yet, join a community different from you as they gather to read Scripture. Perhaps a church filled with people from another denomination or ethnicity. You might begin to see things in the biblical text (and in yourself) you were completely blind to before, such as when Sue and I read the Bible with Mt. Zion Missionary Baptist Church in Los Angeles.

A Christmas Story

One Christmas, Sue and I discovered the true power of *Lectio Alius* around our own dining room table. Christmas Eve found the Stratton family engaging in a decades-old family tradition— reading the Christmas story aloud. Our tradition calls for a script pieced together from the various Christmas passages across the Gospels and then read in rotation by each participant one paragraph at a time. It is a beautiful practice. Only this Christmas Eve was unlike any other.

As we took turns reading our assigned passages, we came to a portion of the Christmas story most families skip—Herod's genocide of Bethlehem's children (Matt. 2:16–18). That night, this heinous paragraph fell to me. My eyes were merely running over the page as I recited a familiar story. However, as I read, I sensed the growing tension in the young woman sitting beside me—my daughter's friend Sandra Uwiringiyimana. Sandra was born to the Banyamulenge people—one of the many minority tribes in the Democratic Republic of the Congo. In the summer of 2004, another larger tribe targeted her small Christian tribe for genocide.

Fearing for their lives, her family fled to a United Nations refugee camp in Burundi. Their attackers followed.

In August of 2004, Sandra's baby sister, her cousin, and countless extended family members and friends were massacred in a single night. What's worse, their attackers were professing Christians as well. I won't write what we talked about that night, but Sandra wrote in her memoir, *How Dare the Sun Rise*:

> I heard our attackers singing and chanting . . . Christian songs. I had grown up singing some of those songs in church, and I wondered why murderers would be singing them. "Imana yabatugabiye," the men chanted. "God has given you to us." The men seemed to think they were on a mission from God to massacre us.[32]

As Sandra shared her story, we all *felt* the deep sorrow in the Christmas story we had never before imagined without her presence. Our compassion for her family, her tribe, and suffering believers everywhere increased exponentially. We also saw ourselves and our American Christian tribalism in a light that shook us to the core. Was the American church already on a path that could one day lead to us committing such atrocities against fellow believers in Jesus's name? It was a night none of us will ever forget. Such is the power of other-centered **Love** unlocked by *Lectio Alius*.

*Scan the QR code below for the backstory on Gary's climb toward **Love**.*

*Scan the QR code below for a special story about learning to **Love** for couples.*

EIGHT

EMBODIMENT

Green Bean Pancakes

"When they saw him, they worshiped him, though some doubted. Then Jesus said to them, 'All authority in heaven and on earth has been given to me. Therefore, make disciples of all peoples as you go, baptizing them in the name of the Father, and of the Son, and of the Holy Spirit, and teaching them to follow everything I have taught you. For surely I am with you always, to the very end of the age.'"

—Matthew 28:17–20 GDS

On May 29, 1953, Sherpa Tenzing Norgay guided New Zealander Edmund Hillary to 28,835 feet—even higher than Tenzing had led the Swiss expedition a year earlier.[1] Less than two hundred vertical feet from Everest's summit, they stood side by side staring up at the same forty-foot cliff likely faced by George Mallory and Sandy Irvine the day they fell to their deaths. Undaunted, Hillary wedged himself into a crack in the rock and slowly inched his way up like Santa climbing a chimney. After an hour of exhausting climbing, the former beekeeper reached the top of the cliff known forever after as "Hillary's Step." The New Zealander threw the Sherpa a rope, then belayed Tenzing while he ascended the cliff. Less than an hour of labored trudging later, Tenzing Norgay and Edmund Hillary accomplished a feat once considered impossible—the world's first confirmed summit of Mount Everest.

In a remarkable historical coincidence, word of Tenzing and Hillary's success reached England on the morning of the coronation of Queen Elizabeth II. Her Majesty's courtiers seized upon the achievement as a symbol of the strength of the British Empire and a token of God's favor upon their new queen. They ensured that one of Elizabeth's first royal decrees proclaimed Hillary "Knight Commander of the Order of the British Empire."[2]

Tragically, the Queen's advisers exploited uncertainty over Tenzing's nationality as an excuse for not knighting the Sherpa as well.[3] Their decision contributed to a worldwide controversy. Europe celebrated Hillary as the first to summit Everest, while Asia celebrated Tenzing. Incredibly, the controversy never broke the lifelong bond between the two climbers. They remained as roped together in their fame as on their climb. Each resisted pressure from politicians and journalists to claim the singular crown of "the first human to summit Everest." Instead, each insisted they reached the top "together."[4]

An Incomplete Metaphor

It may be hard to see how Tenzing and Hillary's achievement directly correlates to the spiritual journey of Jesus's followers. Has *any* student of Jesus throughout human history ever reached some unsurpassable summit of human discipleship? Probably not. The only spiritual climber to ever conquer the summit of perfectly loving God and neighbor was Jesus. While the physical mountain he climbed—Golgotha[5]—stood less than 2,600 vertical feet above sea level, its spiritual elevation was, for all practical purposes, infinite. From the great drops of blood he sweat in his **Prayer** of complete **Surrender** to his heavenly Father's **Desire** in the garden of Gethsemane[6] to the blood he shed on the cross, Jesus's perfect **Love** made him the first and perhaps only spiritual climber in human history who could rightfully cry out, "It is finished!" (John 19:30).

Theologians continue to debate the theological meaning of the atonement Jesus accomplished in his willing sacrifice. Did he: (1) ransom humanity from Satan's power, (2) exemplify the love of God and neighbor at any cost, (3) perfectly satisfy God's demand for justice, or (4) serve as a sinless substitute for the death penalty humanity so richly deserves for our sin? Each theory contains a profound kernel of truth. Each falls short of a complete explanation when pushed to its logical conclusion. What the Gospel accounts do make clear is that, through his death and resurrection, Jesus ascended to his Father not only as the redeemer of Israel but also as the risen Lord of heaven and earth.[7] *That* is a summit no disciple will ever approach.

Tenzing and the Sherpa as Teachers

Yet, considering Tenzing Norgay's life after summiting Everest, the Jesus Climb metaphor still proves helpful. While he continued climbing mountains, Tenzing devoted his life to *teaching* a new generation of mountaineers. Less than six months after successfully climbing Everest, Tenzing cofounded the Himalayan Mountaineering Institute near his home in Darjeeling, India. Tenzing and his band of Sherpa instructors developed the climbing curriculum now used in mountaineering schools worldwide. While the United Kingdom never did knight him, Tenzing's global chain of learning grew so extensive that *Time* magazine declared him "one of the 100 most influential people of the twentieth century."[8]

Teach the World What You Learned from Me

Similarly, the Gospel writers are careful to impress upon their readers that even though Jesus's climb was complete, his work on earth was not. John tells us Jesus instructed his disciples, "As the Father has sent me, I am sending you" (20:21). Mark relates that Jesus taught his students: "Go into all the world and preach the gospel to all creation" (16:15). Luke tells us he called them to be witnesses to everything they learned and saw in him so that "repentance for the forgiveness of sins will be preached in his name to all nations, beginning at Jerusalem" (24:47).

These final instructions, commonly called Jesus's Great Commission, find their most famous formulation in Matthew's Gospel:

> All authority in heaven and on earth has been given to me. Therefore, make disciples of all peoples as you go, baptizing them in the name of the Father, and of the Son, and of the Holy Spirit, and teaching them to follow everything I have taught you. For surely I am with you always, to the very end of the age. (28:18–20 GDS)

Jesus commissioning his disciples to teach others breaks no new ground. All Jewish rabbis labored for the day when they released their students to become teachers. As I mentioned in Chapter One (**Desire**), a common saying among rabbis of the era was, "He who has students who in turn have students of their own is called Rabbi." As one world-renowned rabbinic scholar affirms, "Each begins as a disciple of a master, then himself becomes a master to the next generation of disciples, in a long chain of learning."[9] Every rabbi's goal was to transform their nation by transforming their students. "According to the Rabbinic ideal, all of Israel would be teachers, and ultimately masters, of Torah."[10] Only then could Jewish society reflect the Torah's call for justice, charitable acts, gifts of first fruits, and sacrifices.

Jesus's charge to his disciples perfectly aligns with this tradition while vastly increasing its scope. A commission from your rabbi to be a teacher in Israel is one thing, but Jesus calls his ragtag band of xenophobic fishermen, tax collectors, and zealots to start an educational movement capable of teaching the entire *world*.

You can easily imagine Peter chuckling, "Ha-ha, Lord. That's a good one."

John the Beloved would join him in the joke (from Jesus's side, of course) until he noticed Jesus wasn't laughing. Then he would motion for Peter's attention and whisper, "Uh, Pete. I think he's serious."

To which Peter, John, and every student in Jesus's climbing school must have spilled their lattes as they spluttered, "Wait, what?"

Of course, it didn't happen exactly that way. Still, Jesus's commission must have marked the exact moment when his disciples finally recognized their Teacher's genius in starting a "college" before establishing his church. Their Teacher's goal was not to create warring tribal gatherings fearfully holding on to their members. He intended the kingdom of God to fill the earth through a movement of climbing schools capable of selecting, training, and releasing their "graduates" to go forth into their world as teachers.

Embodiment

Remarkably, the Great Commission encapsulates nearly every element of the Twelve's three-year journey of following Jesus from student to disciple. In commissioning them to "make disciples" by "teaching" the nations, Jesus echoes his initial call to **Desire** him as their teacher. By commissioning them to baptize their students, he echoes his call to repent ("rethink their thinking") under his kingdom **Instruction**. In commissioning them to teach their students to "follow everything I have taught have you," he echoes his call to **Surrender** their lesser desires in exchange for the kingdom of God. In entrusting his commission to the disciples as a group and not merely as individuals, Jesus permanently ropes them (and us) together in a self-perpetuating educational **Community**.

In commissioning his disciples with the promise, "I am with you always, to the very end of the age," Jesus reassured his students that the **Intimacy** they enjoyed with him during his earthly ministry would only *increase* as they established climbing colleges around the world. In rooting his commission in the postresurrection reality of possessing "all authority in heaven and on earth," Jesus echoes his call for the disciple's to **Pray** that God's "will be done on earth as it is in heaven." His commission to teach everything he taught echoes his call to observe his greatest commandment to **Love** God and neighbor.

The continual upward/downward journey back and forth between these expedition camps leads to the final expedition camp on the journey from student to disciple: **Embodiment**. Remember, when rabbis spoke of a "chain of learning" they hoped to forge, they were not speaking of the mere transmission of information into a student's mind. They were speaking of the transformation of a student's life. As discussed in Chapter One (**Desire**), a true rabbi was considered the "Torah transformed into an embodied form of human being."[11]

Jesus shares this goal. He did not call his disciples to go into the world as salespeople seeking to close a deal. In the same way he **Embodied** the eternal Word in his incarnation—"The Word became flesh and made his dwelling among us" (John 1:14)—Jesus expected his disciples to become the **Embodiment** of his teachings and way of life among the nations. This was how they were to "make disciples."

Embodying Jesus's Teachings to a City

Few disciples in American history modeled the power of **Embodiment** quite like Sarah Osborn (1714–96). Colonial era customs forbade women to vote, attend college, or enter the ministry. Yet Osborn became the de facto spiritual leader of her Newport, Rhode Island, church and one of her generation's most well-known religious leaders. Widowed at age nineteen (1733) with a one-year-old son, Sarah turned to one of the few occupations available for a single mother to support herself: schoolteacher. A gifted and creative instructor, Sarah's students thrived. But when an economic downturn forced her to close her school, she faced crushing poverty while struggling with depression and suicidal ideation. Her once strong faith wavered and nearly faltered.

Things began to change when the First Great Awakening swept through New England in 1740–41. The two greatest preachers of the Awakening—George Whitefield and Gilbert Tennent—visited Newport and deeply impacted Osborn, as did the writings of Jonathan Edwards, the greatest theologian of the Awakening. As her faith strengthened, Sarah submitted to God's call to move beyond mere personal piety and devote her life to spiritual **Community**. With reassurance from God, "Go forward. Fear not, for I am with thee," she accepted the marriage proposal of a widower nearly thirty years her senior.

The marriage provided Sarah and her son with a stable home for the first time in their life, but it wasn't long before tragedy struck again. First, her beloved son suddenly passed away. Then, her new husband's poor business decisions led the couple into bankruptcy, wiping out Sarah's carefully gathered savings. Forced to return to teaching to support her new family, Sarah opened a school in her living room. When tuition payments from her students proved insufficient to avoid eviction from her rented home, she offered room and board for older scholars preparing for admission to New England's only two colleges: Harvard and Yale. Moved by the plight of Newport's slaves (nearly 17 percent of the city's population), Sarah initiated classes for Black boys and girls and their parents. Soon, women across Newport and throughout New England began to look to her for spiritual guidance. And then their husbands did as well. When her pastor descended into alcoholism, Osborn became the de facto spiritual leader of her church.

Osborn's home pulsed with life as the **Community** she fostered among her seventy daytime students and more than sixty women in evening "spiritual societies" became the source of spiritual transformation for many. When God answered the **Prayers** of these women with a revival in 1761, over five hundred people began attending classes or meetings in Sarah's home *every week*— men and women, Black and White, rich and poor.[12] Osborn was the first woman in the history of the American colonies to lead such as revival, but her pioneering example blazed a climbing trail for many to follow.

As her physical strength began to fail, Osborn prevailed upon the elders of her church to hire Jonathan Edward's protégé, Samuel Hopkins, as their new pastor, guaranteeing that those entrusted to her spiritual care would be in safe hands. Sarah helped open Hopkins's eyes to the evils of slavery and rejoiced when he agreed to preach for Newport's first Black church.[13] Hopkins became an early leader in the movement to abolish slavery and in 1776 became the first person to petition Congress to free all enslaved people.[14]

Through poverty, revivals, grief, and the spiritual care of so many, Sarah wrote down everything. Inspired by the "case studies" in Jonathan Edwards's work, Osborn began a memoir detailing her spiritual journey in the hope of helping others on their journeys. It was one of the first and only memoirs written by an English-speaking woman of the era. The spiritual depth and emotional poignancy of her writing gripped all who read it, especially her honesty regarding her struggles and doubts. By the end of her life, Sarah had written over fifty additional volumes of notes and diaries. After her death, Rev. Hopkins published much of her work, and the *Memoirs of the Life of Mrs. Sarah Osborn* became a best-selling volume for decades.[15] More than fifty years after her death, influential Presbyterian minister Gardiner Spring (1785–1873) added Osborn to the pantheon of Christian luminaries—such as John Owen and Richard Baxter—who lived lives of "splendid examples of moral excellence [and] whose light will shine through a long line of succeeding generations."[16]

Economic scholars today regard Osborn as a "prophet" of **Community** and altruism versus selfishness and greed, "a person of piety and true virtue, one who lived not for self but others."[17] Her **Embodiment** of the Great Commission helped lay the foundation for a Second Great Awakening that was far more other-centered and **Community**-oriented than the First Great Awakening. The example of her Newport woman's society helped birth a vast network of Christian voluntary associations intent upon tackling social problems of their city. They worked to abolish slavery and "reform bankruptcy laws, prison systems, insane asylums, labor laws, and education. They built orphanages and free medical dispensaries and developed programs to provide professional services like social work, job placement, and day camps for children in the slums."[18] Like Tenzing and his mountaineering school, Osborn refused to content herself with merely reaching a summit of personal piety. She sought to *live what Jesus taught and teach what Jesus lived.* In so doing, she **Embodied** her Teacher to a city and her nation.

Discipling Your People

Sarah Osborn's life illustrates the reality that the Greek word often translated as "nations" in the Great Commission designates much more than just the 195 *countries* for which we usually use the word today. A better translation would be "tribe" or "people." This means that the heart of the Great Commission is Jesus's call to live out his Great Commandments among a people. Discipling nations may seem like a far-fetched goal. But make no mistake, Jesus has a *people* he is calling you to disciple—a people who may not ever be discipled if you refuse to **Embody** and share Jesus's teachings in their midst. It could be a family, a neighborhood, a church, a team, a city, a nation, a workplace, or all the above.

For example, Amy Sherman warns that many "Christians simply turn off their faith at work; they function as practical atheists on the job. They have no vision for what it means to partner with God at work, to . . . accomplish kingdom purposes in and through their work."[19] Our Teacher's vision calls us to make "disciples—students, apprentices, practitioners—of Jesus Christ, steadily learning from him how to live the life of the Kingdom of the Heavens into every corner of human existence."[20] As biblical scholar N. T. Wright reminds us, "The gospel of Jesus points us and indeed urges us to be at the leading edge of the whole culture, . . . story and music and art and philosophy and education and poetry and politics."[21]

Academy Award-Winning Screenwriter

For instance, Randall Wallace sensed his Teacher's commission to build upon Jesus's teaching by creating film and television capable of inspiring audiences to live ethically and lead nobly. Yet his journey to follow that call had led him to the brink of financial ruin. After some initial success, a Hollywood writer's strike left him in danger of losing his house, his family, and his mind. One day Randall could go no further. Watching his hands tremble as he tried to write, he feared he was suffering a nervous breakdown like his father. He dropped to his knees in his office and prayed a prayer of **Surrender** not unlike Jesus's prayer in the garden of Gethsemane: "My Father, if it is possible, may this cup be taken from me. Yet not as I will, but as you will" (Matt. 26:39).

Out of that heart-rending hour of prayer, God reassured Randall of his love and calling. As he dried his tears, a story his grandmother once told him about one of his ancestors came to mind. The ancestor's name was William Wallace. Randall got up off the floor of his office and wrote the first lines of the screenplay we now know as the film *Braveheart*.[22] The film saved Randall Wallace's career and won an Academy Award for Best Picture. Randall's **Embodiment** of Jesus's teaching through his "secular" film career[23] fulfilled Jesus's calling to "disciple nations."

Personalizing the Great Commission

Allowing Jesus to personalize the Great Commission for our lives is crucial to our **Embodiment** of his teachings and his way of life. Frederick Buechner wisely suggests, "The place God calls you to is the place where your deep gladness and the world's deep hunger meet."[24] This means we don't necessarily need to go to the ends of the earth to find deep needs. They are all around us.

Deep Needs

As Jesus explains in the parable of the sheep and goats (Matt. 25:31–46), entrance into the kingdom of God comes to those who meet the deep needs of the people in their sphere of influence. "I was hungry and you gave me something to eat, I was thirsty and you gave me something to drink, I was a stranger and you invited me in, I needed clothes and you clothed me, I was sick and you looked after me, I was in prison and you came to visit me. . . . Truly I tell you, whatever you did for one of the least of these brothers and sisters of mine, you did for me" (vv. 35–36, 40).

Jesus makes a similar point in the parable of the good Samaritan (Luke 10:25–37). He closes the loophole on a religious leader seeking a limit to his responsibility to love his neighbor. Jesus's story of a despised Samaritan meeting the needs of a traveler waylaid by bandits reminds the leader that religious, cultural, ethnic, and racial differences are no excuse for failing to show mercy to those in need. This is often an acid test of "other-centered" love: Can we invite people into our lives when they are different from us or when there is little in it for us? Jesus instructed his followers, "When you give a banquet, invite the poor, the crippled, the lame, the blind . . . although they cannot repay you" (Luke 14:12–14). It may take hard work to learn to see past the blindness of our self-interest long enough to see the deep needs around us. But once we do, we've taken our first step toward becoming bearers of God's healing to a broken world.

Deep Gladness

The second element in Buechner's maxim, discovering our "deep gladness," also takes effort. Too many people settle for a safe career when Jesus beckons us forward into his wild and intimate calling. Quaker educator Parker Palmer insists, "Before you tell your life what you intend to do with it, listen for what it intends to do with you."[25] As Howard Thurman, dean of the chapel at Howard University, counseled his students, "Don't ask yourself what the world needs. Ask yourself what makes you come alive, and go do that, because what the world needs is people who have come alive."[26]

This element often involves discerning our "role" more than our "people." For instance, I knew for years that my "people" were students and those who teach and lead them. But my sacred/secular thinking prevented me from seeking any other role than "professional ministry." Even when I was miserable in a campus ministry role for which I was ill-suited, I refused to consider other options. Such perseverance may have strengthened my character, but I also spent years fighting depression. (Scan the QR code at the end of the chapter to learn that story.) Then a chance encounter landed me the role of a part-time high school teacher. I came home from my first day in the classroom full of such deep gladness that I thought I might explode. I came through the door and announced to Sue, "I finally found my calling."

Discernment

This means there are two sides to Buechner's equation: gladness and need. Lean too far into focusing on the world's deep needs, and you may find yourself grinding away serving a people or in a role God never intended for you. Lean too far toward satisfying only your own gladness, and you may serve only yourself. This makes discerning God's call on our lives a bit of a balancing act. How do we know if we are meeting real needs or if our joy is self-centered? This is where the power of Jesus's teaching **Embodied** in an entire **Community** becomes so essential. Jesus often confirms his personalization of the Great Commission *through* the people he's called us to serve.

A Climbing Guide for the Disciple's Descent into
EMBODIMENT

Obviously, becoming an **Embodiment** of Jesus's teachings and way of life to your **Community** takes a lifetime, but here are a two practices that might help you get started.

Connecting Your World's Deep Needs to Your Great, Deep Gladness

Seek Jesus for his personalizing of the Great Commission in your life. Use your journal or phone to make two columns: "Things I

Love Doing" and "Things I Care About." In the first column, write down everything that comes into your mind that you love to do. It could be a hobby, sport, favorite subject, activity, accomplishment, or experience; *anything* that brings you great joy. In the second column, write down every cause, need, or news story you deeply care about. Values you hold. Needs that keep you up at night. News headlines you always click. Videos that make you cry.

Now, prayerfully look through your lists to find items in your first column that connect with an item from the second. For instance, maybe you wrote *baby goats* in your "Things I Care About" list and *babysitting* in your "Things I Love Doing" list. You might have discovered a people with a deep need that would be a great joy for you to meet—goat farmers! Maybe you could start a ministry to goat farmers (or find a job) babysitting baby goats? It sounds silly initially, but if you spend time prayerfully working on your lists, you may discover something of Jesus's personalization of the Great Commission in your life. I would recommend this process for choosing a career or a major as well.

Discern Your People

Once you begin to comprehend how God has wired you to meet the needs of others, try to discern who those "others" might be. Don't look too far off into the future or to another place. Don't allow social media's overwhelming stream of deep and compelling needs from around the globe paralyze your current local efforts. (And don't kid yourself into thinking that posting on social media about a need in Washington or Zimbabwe is the same as other-centered service in your locality.)

Now, prayerfully seek others in your community gripped by meeting the same need and join their efforts. Whether you rope yourself to a nonprofit, a business, a church, a community, or a student group, you need climbing partners to help you on your journey of other-centered service. Don't fall into the trap of think-ing your life is so busy now that you need to wait until later to devote part of each week to serving the people God has placed in your life. If your goal is to join Jesus in his mission to set the world right by working and praying for his kingdom to come and his will to be done on earth, then you need to start now. And here's the beautiful thing: once you've discerned your people, God often uses that same **Community** to confirm your calling. That's what happened for Sue and me.

An Unexpected Calling

Plans for Wheaton in Watts were already well underway when Sue and I arrived back in Wheaton after honeymooning over Christmas break. We had deliberately saved up enough money that neither of us needed to get a job for the first month of our life together. We wanted sufficient free time to focus on building a solid foundation for our marriage. Our plan then called for both of us to get jobs, me part-time and Sue full-time. What we didn't anticipate was how our responsibilities around Wheaton in Watts would explode.

We had group meetings four nights per week. Plus, Sue led two weekly small groups of Wheaton students who had asked her to "disciple" them, complete with one-on-one mentoring for each student. Oh yeah, and I was taking a full-time load of demanding senior classes, including Greek V (after skipping Greek IV). It was our great joy to meet the deep needs of our "people," but it was also exhausting. How on earth were we ever going to add jobs on top of all this?

The crisis came to a head the night after Sue's interview with a local law firm went exceptionally well. We should have been ecstatic. Instead, we both grew quiet. Over dinner, I told her, "I'm so proud of you for landing such a great job, but I'm also heartbroken at the thought of everything you will have to give up on campus if you accept it."

"I know," she sighed. "I doubt I'll even be able to go to Los Angeles. That breaks my heart too."

"So why are you taking the job, again?" I asked.

"Because we need to eat," she laughed, throwing her napkin at me. "Your part-time job barely pays for this apartment, and I can't see you doing much more with four classes and everything else you've got going on."

"Yes, we need to eat," I admitted. "But then, why are you ministering on campus?"

Frustrated, she threw up her hands and nearly screamed, "Because our heavenly Father called me to minister to students!"

I nodded and raised my palms in appeasement. "I totally agree."

"So what's your point?" she asked, eyes glistening. (Being a woman called to ministry is not an easy vocation.)

I almost winced as I proposed the thought that had been rattling around in my head all day, "What if your *job* was to minister on campus?"

She dropped her head and rubbed her temples as she slowly posited, "And who is going to pay?"

"Our heavenly Father?" I offered.

Suddenly, Sue became very quiet. I knew this was either an excellent development or a very bad one. She got up from the table, walked into our bedroom, and returned with her Bible. She opened it and said, "I read these verses this morning: 'Do not worry, saying, "What shall we eat?" or "What shall we drink?" or "What shall we wear?" For . . . your heavenly Father knows that you need them. But seek first his kingdom and his righteousness, and all these things will be given to you as well'" (Matt. 6:31–33).

She closed her Bible and continued, "As I read these verses, I felt like God somehow reassured me that we could trust him to provide for us if we keep doing what we're doing on campus. Is that crazy?"

"Yes, it's crazy," I replied. "But that's what I'm sensing too."

"So how do we do this?" She gulped.

"Maybe we should write up some sort of a contract," I suggested.

"Why don't we just pray," she countered.

"That's a better idea," I admitted. So we prayed something like, "Lord, we believe you called Sue into this unexpected and fruitful ministry to these students. We will trust you to provide for her ministry as reliably as a paycheck until the day comes when we don't have food on the table. In Jesus's name, amen."

Green Bean Pancakes

So Sue turned down the position with the law firm, and we tightened our belts for a season of frugal living. We didn't care. We were young and in love. Plus, we were caught up in the wonder of all God was doing before and after Watts. (See the QR code at the end of this chapter for the whole story.) We didn't have a car, so every morning we walked the mile from our apartment to campus to minister and study. Every evening, we walked the mile home to our apartment, sharing everything we experienced together and apart that day. Along the way, we would stop at the grocery store across the train tracks from our apartment and purchase what we needed with whatever money we had.

Until the night the money ran out. I mean no cash, no savings, nothing in my student account. Zero! As we walked *past* the grocery store, I tried to put on a brave face, telling Sue, "Well, at least it's not terrible timing."

"How's that?" she asked.

"We don't have any bills due tomorrow."

"Yeah," Sue replied. "But we also don't have anything to eat tonight."

Then she reconsidered, "Actually, we have pancake mix and a can of green beans."

I forced a laugh and quipped, "Then I guess we'll have green bean pancakes for dinner." But I wasn't laughing on the inside. Inside, I was dying, as my Dementors began howling, "You heard God wrong. You are such a loser."

We climbed the three flights of stairs up to our apartment in the silence of heartbreak. As we rounded the last corner of the hallway, I noticed something odd—a grocery bag in front of our apartment door.

We peered inside. It was full of groceries.

Wide-eyed, Sue whispered, "Is this for us?"

Looking furtively up and down the hall, I blurted, "It is now!"

We put the bag on the kitchen table to carefully examine its contents. Whoever filled it knew us well. There were pretzels for me and Oreos for Sue. We started dancing around the kitchen like toddlers on a sugar high.

A phone call broke our reverie. It was the Cru campus director, Jim. "Hey," he said. "Someone left something for you in our apartment. Can you come get it?" (He lived in the building next door.)

It was another bag of groceries. "Wow!" We squealed.

Jim smiled, "Well if you like that, you're going to love this." Then he opened his refrigerator to reveal *another* bag of groceries. Our mouths dropped open, but before we could speak, Jim opened his freezer to show us yet *another* bag. This one even had a frozen steak and a gallon of ice cream.

Now Sue and I were crying. I mean snot running down your face, tears blinding your eyes crying. We hugged Jim (of course, he, Steve, Jan, and the other Wheaton in Watts-ers had organized all this) and voiced our eternal gratitude.

"I don't know what you're talking about," he winked.

We stumbled back to our apartment carrying three grocery bags (from three different stores), singing praise songs to our God. But as we came around the last corner to our apartment, we saw . . . three *more* bags of groceries sitting in front of our door.

It was so much food and so well coordinated that it fed us for the rest of the term. We even saved the steak to have something special to serve my mom and dad when they visited for my graduation. My dad chewed happily as my mom asked, "So, Sue, how's that job going?"

Sue choked, shot me a panicked glance, then recovered with a perfect deadpan, "Best boss and coworkers I've ever had!"

A Beloved Community

And they were. Of all the miracles surrounding that year, nothing compares to the intimate Father care of God expressed by the beautiful Wheaton in Watts **Community**. (And they didn't stop with groceries. Checks and cash kept showing up in our mailbox for weeks.) We laid down part of our lives to **Embody** the Great Commission by seeking to meet the needs of our "people." Our "people"—our **Community**—**Embodied** Jesus's teaching by laying down their lives to help meet our deep needs.

Since that time, Sue and I have spent our lives together seeking to meet the deep needs of our people—students and those who teach and lead them. And those students, faculty, staff, and student ministers have been a constant source of unspeakable joy for us. Yet we sometimes wonder who we would have become if fear had kept us from serving our people and making space for our people to serve us and confirm our calling in the most unexpected way. We can't claim to have changed our city like Sarah Osborn (or Hollywood like Randall Wallace), but we have known the deep joy of seeing Jesus reveal his love to thousands of students in classrooms, dorm rooms, living rooms, film rooms, coffee shops, and service trips. Through it all we've sought to *teach what Jesus lived* and *live what Jesus taught* in everything we do. This is the **Embodiment** of Jesus's Great Commission: to make disciples by baptizing and teaching them to follow everything Jesus taught, especially his greatest commandment and highest summit to love God and others with everything we are.

*Scan the QR code below for the backstory on Gary's climb toward **Embodiment**.*

EPILOGUE

"You did not choose me, but I chose you and appointed you so that you might go and bear fruit—*fruit that will last*—and so that whatever you ask in my name the Father will give you. This is my command: Love each other."

—Jesus of Nazareth (John 15:16–17—italics mine)

Lene Gammelgaard refused to make *summiting* Mount Everest her goal. While she pushed herself daily with the mantra, "Train harder. Climb longer," she never lost sight of the fact that most climbers who perish on Everest do so on the way *down*. So instead of covering her workout room wall with inspirational photos of Everest's summit, she posted a single photo of Hillary's Step. On the image, she printed in giant letters: "To the summit and safe return!"[1]

Her focus saved her life. After a year of training, a month of acclimatization, and a week of hard climbing, Gammelgaard achieved her life dream of standing on the rooftop of the world. She found herself "quietly, silently, massively content."

She was also impossibly tired.

So instead of lingering on the summit, she posed for an obligatory photo, threw her camera into her backpack, and headed straight for base camp. She told herself, "Maybe I'll have to climb [Everest] again to enjoy the view or have enough strength left to notice that there is [a view]. It is too much now. I just want to get down safely. . . . And that can't happen fast enough."[2]

Moments after she cleared Hillary's Step, a massive blizzard struck the mountainside. The storm claimed the lives of eight of Gammelgaard's climbing partners. She lived to tell her summit story because she set her sights not merely on the summit but on *continuing* her journey.

This is my undying hope for you as well. We start the Jesus Climb as students. We complete it as disciples. All we need to do is *continue* on our journey. My deepest prayer for you is that you will not lose heart. Junko Tabei, the first woman to summit Everest, famously described her secret to climbing the world's tallest mountain as something beyond ability and technique: "No matter how slow a person walks, they can still reach the summit, one step at a time."[3] As Rocky Balboa tells the young Adonis Creed: "One step at a time. One punch at a time. One round at a time. Every champion was once a contender that refused to give up."[4] This is how you win fights. (At least in *Rocky* movies.) This is how you climb mountains. This is how you follow Jesus from student to disciple: you don't give up.

Maturity Not Perfection

Yet please don't confuse persistence with sinless perfection. It seems unlikely Jesus would instruct his disciples to pray daily for the forgiveness of their sins if he didn't expect them to sin more or less daily. As John Calvin warns, it is a "devilish invention . . . to be cocksure of one's own perfection."[5] Near the end of his life, John the Beloved wrote his disciples, "If we claim to be without sin, we deceive ourselves and the truth is not in us. If we confess our sins, he is faithful and just and will forgive us our sins and purify us from all unrighteousness" (1 John 1:8–9).[6] The Jesus of the Gospels seems more than willing to pick us up each time we've fallen, dust us off, and send us back for another round in our fight, another leg of our climb.

If John Wesley is correct, maturity in our upward/downward journey may even make it possible for mere mortals to climb to such spiritual heights that the "habitual disposition of our soul" becomes distinguished by "the humble, gentle, patient love of God and our neighbor, ruling our tempers, words, and actions."[7] No one climbs to such spiritual heights quickly, nor without securing the bottled oxygen of grace flowing into their souls. Yet this is the goal of our Jesus Climb. We may never *dwell* on the summit of perfect discipleship, yet Jesus seems to encourage us to believe it is at least possible for an occasional visit.

Your Jesus Climb

Of course, I have no way of knowing your current location on your Jesus Climb. You could be just taking your first tentative steps out of base camp. You may be powering through the death zone on your way toward your third summit attempt. Odds are you are someplace in between. And remember, since we're always on a journey of ascent and descent at the same time, you may find yourself approaching more than one camp at any given moment. The one thing I know for certain is that Jesus—who knows you better than you know yourself—has already created a personalized climbing plan for you and walks beside you even now.

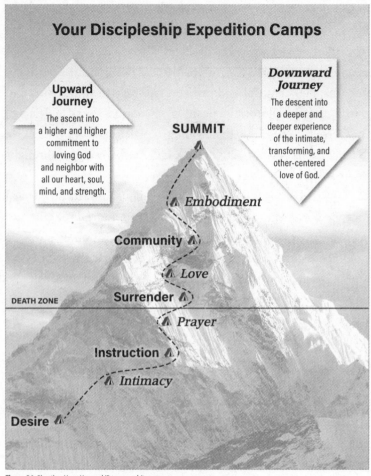

Figure 9.1. Charting Your Upward/Downward Journey

So my recommendation for making the best use of this book would be for you to look back over the expedition camps discussed in the previous chapters as you ask Jesus for the wisdom to discern your current location (or locations). Then reread that chapter a few times, meditate on Jesus's teaching passages in that chapter, and start implementing at least one of the practices described in its climbing guide. Don't worry if *you* can't discern which camp you are currently climbing toward (or descending to); *every* disciple visits *every* expedition camp many different times over the course of their spiritual journey. So, if you don't know where you are, just pick a camp that interests you and dig in further.

If you've continued reading this far, you almost certainly possess true spiritual summit fever. So, allow me to close our journey together with the stories of two final students who continued following Jesus determinedly enough to at least catch sight of the summit of genuine discipleship.

Mary Magdalene

Few disciples demonstrated persistence like Mary Magdalene. Rescued from a life dominated by demonic evil, Mary grew into someone capable of incredible courage. Unlike most of the Twelve, she followed Jesus all the way to the cross. Unlike *any* of the Twelve, she risked the wrath of Roman guards to prepare Jesus's body for burial. And Mary Magdalene alone remained at the empty tomb to weep over the disappearance of Jesus's body.

Her determination bore incredible fruit when Jesus allowed her to become the first person to witness his resurrection from the dead! Not surprisingly, when he called her name, "Mary," she turned toward him and cried out in Aramaic, "Rabbouni!" (which means "my own dear *teacher*"). Long before he ever gave the Great Commission to the Twelve, Jesus commissioned Mary, "Go . . . to my brothers and tell them, 'I am ascending to my Father and your Father, to my God and your God'" (John 20:17).

It should have been the most triumphant moment in the history of Jesus's climbing school. Instead, the Twelve met Mary's declaration, "He is risen," not with belief but skepticism. Mark tells us, "She went and told those who had been with him and who were mourning and weeping. When they heard that Jesus was alive and that she had seen him, *they did not believe it*"

(Mark 16:10–11—italics mine). Despite her initial disappointment, Mary Magdalene's faithfulness in fulfilling Jesus's commission sparked Peter and John the Beloved to seek the truth. They ran to the empty tomb to investigate for themselves, and shortly after that, Jesus revealed himself to them as well.

Thomas

Thomas also demonstrates persistence, but not nearly so consistently as Mary. Chosen by Jesus as one of the Twelve apostles, Thomas somehow managed to miss the most extraordinary event in human history: the resurrection of Jesus. When the other disciples tell him they have seen the Lord, he is forthright in his doubt: "Unless I see the nail marks in his hands and put my finger where the nails were, and put my hand into his side, I will not believe" (John 20:25).

His spiritual honesty earns him the nickname "Doubting Thomas," which seems completely unfair. None of the other disciples believed Mary Magdalene's account of meeting the risen Jesus until they too saw the wounds in his body themselves. Why should Thomas be singled out for his doubt?

Fortunately for Thomas, Jesus was more than willing to address his skepticism. When he finally appeared to Thomas, Jesus reassured him, "Put your finger here; see my hands. Reach out your hand and put it into my side. Stop doubting and believe" (John 20:27). Thomas's honesty pays off in a big way, with actual experiential knowledge instead of mere notional understanding. And many view his response to Jesus, "My Lord and my God!" (20:28), as one of the clearest examples of the disciple's early understanding of Jesus's divinity.

Not surprisingly, Thomas proceeded to travel further than any of the other disciples in his passion for continuing on the journey for which Jesus commissioned him. He took trading ships to India, where he preached the gospel of the kingdom in Kerala province and was martyred outside Chennai, India. He is the only one of Jesus's Twelve apostles buried in a marked grave. Having personally stood on the Mount of St. Thomas, you can almost feel the passion of Thomas's three-thousand-plus mile journey from Jerusalem, driven by the white-hot love for his Teacher and his hope of helping set the world right.

A Journey of Worship and Doubt

I recall Thomas's and Mary's stories here because they demonstrate the internal and external setbacks every disciple faces on their journey. All true disciples worship and witness. All true disciples question and doubt. I hope you find that comforting. Stubborn unbelief is clearly questionable. Honestly expressing your doubts is not. Perhaps this is why Matthew's account of the Great Commission carefully noted the mixed reaction of the disciples who encountered the risen Jesus: "When they saw him, they worshiped him; but some doubted" (Matt. 28:17). Matthew insists that those who set out to fulfill their teacher's call to teach everyone, everywhere, everything he taught will do so as part of a community of both faith and doubt. No perfect disciples need apply.

The hidden lesson of these resurrection appearances points to the reality that expressing our doubts to safe people (and becoming a safe person for others) is one of the hallmarks of a Great Commission **Community**. Doubt is part of the educational process, not necessarily the enemy. Genuine repentance—rethinking our thinking—isn't possible without constantly questioning our current (and always incomplete) understanding of Jesus and his kingdom. And how can Jesus address our questions if we won't admit to them? What matters is that we remain in **Community** and **Intimacy** with Jesus whenever we face both our doubts and those of others. As Jesus assures his disciples immediately following his

Great Commission, "And surely I am with you always, to the very end of the age" (Matt. 28:20).

The Fruit of Persistence

This brings me back to my prayer for you. Like Lene Gammelgaard, I pray that you will set your sights on *completing* your journey. In the parable of the four soils (Luke 8:13–15; also Mark 4:1–20; Matt. 13:1–23), Jesus describes the difference between those who only begin to follow him and those who finish their discipleship journey. Some students are like seed that falls upon rocky soil. They receive Jesus's teaching on the kingdom of God with joy, but because they have no root, "They believe only for a while, but in the time of testing they fall away" (Luke 8:13). Others are like seed that falls among thorns, which are the ones who hear but whose growth is "choked by life's worries, riches and pleasures, and they do not mature" (v. 14). Yet some are like seed that falls upon good soil that bears a *hundredfold return*. These are the ones who, when they hear the word, hold it fast in an honest and good heart and bear fruit with endurance (v. 15). My prayer is that by "persistence in doing good" (Rom. 2:7), you will live a life of hundredfold fruitfulness that will last into all eternity.

On the last night they were together, Jesus told his first students, "You did not choose me, but I chose you and appointed you so that you might go and bear fruit—*fruit that will last*" (John 15:16—italics mine). I believe this is his promise to us as well. If you will only keep following your Teacher on the upward/downward journey toward the summit of loving God and neighbor, something impossible *will* happen, just as it does for every Everest climber committed to the process of acclimatization—far higher in the sky than imagination dared suggest, the white summit of genuine discipleship will finally appear. Through seasons of worship and doubt, testing and temptation, death zone and avalanche, base camp and summit, by the grace of God, you will become a kingdom bearer, a world healer, a disciple of Jesus. As Jesus (and George Mallory) would urge us: the greatest danger is in not daring the adventure.

Scan the QR code below for the culmination of Gary and Sue's student journey.

Scan the QR code below for further resources for continuing your Jesus Climb.

ACKNOWLEDGMENTS

No one climbs, or writes, alone. This book is no exception. My collaborators have been many and varied. First, I want to mention my eternal debt to Michael J. Wilkins, whose tutelage in the meaning of *mathetes* forms the foundation of my understanding of discipleship. I must also express my debt to the late Dallas Willard for his prayers and encouragement over the years, not to mention his lifechanging writings. I also wish to offer special thanks to Barbara Brown Taylor for all her encouragement and the use of her "Approaching the Mountain" prayer. Although I've never had the privilege of meeting him, I must thank John Krakauer, as my impulsive airport bookstore buy of *Into Thin Air* birthed my love of Everest literature so central to this parable. And speaking of births, I want to express my heartfelt gratitude to Kirk McClelland for suggesting I write this book and encouraging me in the project from beginning to end.

Since *The Jesus Climb* began as a sermon series at Gordon College, I wish to thank my Gordon colleagues and students for helping shape these concepts, especially my team-teachers in our Evangelism and Discipleship class: Gary Parrett, Mark Cannister, and Lisa Corry. And since these ideas first became a book at Johnson University, I want to thank my Johnson colleagues and students, especially the faculty, staff, students, and TAs in our First-Year

Student Cornerstone program, as well as the graduate students in Knoxville Fellows class sixteen, for their patience and insight in helping craft multiple drafts over the past few years. In truth, every student and colleague in every discipleship class, retreat, workshop, and lecture I've taught over the years has helped contribute to my understanding of these concepts, especially those at Whittier Christian High School, Biola University, Crown College, Act One Hollywood, Bethel University, Pacific Rim University, Vision New England, the Institute for Campus Revival and Awakening at the Yale Jonathan Edwards Center, the Association of Biblical Higher Education (ABHE), the Council for Christian Colleges and Universities (CCCU), the Society for Professors of Christian Education (SPCE), the Association of Youth Ministry Educators (AYME), the Princeton Theological Seminary Black Seminarians, the Three Rivers Collaborative, the Knoxville Future of Hope Youth Theology Institute, and the Faith and Justice Summit.

My special thanks go to those who helped most in the final formation of the book (and the author), especially Jason Fikes, Aly Hawkins, David Kinnaman, Mary Hardegree, Sandy Armstrong, Emily Mazar, Peter Kapsner, Cara Smith, John Mokkosian, Tim Savaloja, Lem Usita, Scott Reitz, Melissa Larson, Caleb Gilmore, John Lemon, and Mark and Monica Nelson.

The true heroes of this writing project are my remarkable children, Ashley, Jordan, Joshua, and Micaiah, who endured decades of conversations on the meaning of discipleship and who, with the help of my delightful daughters-in-law, Emily and Megan, read countless drafts while encouraging (and prodding) me again and again throughout this odyssey. I could never thank them enough.

Most of all, I wish to thank my precious wife and soulmate, Dr. Susan Lynn Jordan Stratton, for her unconditional love and endless reading (and rereading) of never-ending manuscripts that made this project possible. You truly are the love of my life!

NOTES

Front Matter

[1]George H. Leigh-Mallory, "The Reconnaissance of the Mountain," in C. K. Howard-Bury, *Mount Everest: The Reconnaissance, 1921* (New York: Longmans, Green and Co., 1922), 186.

Preface for Faculty and Campus Leaders

[1]See Gary David Stratton and James L. Gorman, "The Second Great Awakening," in *The Encyclopedia of Christianity in the United States*, vol. 4, ed. George Thomas Kurian and Mark A. Lamport (Lanham, MD: Rowman & Littlefield, 2016), 1011–13. See also Timothy Lawrence Smith, *Revivalism and Social Reform: American Protestantism on the Eve of the Civil War* (Baltimore: Johns Hopkins University Press, 1980); Thomas S. Kidd, *The Great Awakening: The Roots of Evangelical Christianity in Colonial America* (New Haven, CT: Yale University Press, 2009); George M. Marsden, *The Soul of the American University: From Protestant Establishment to Established Nonbelief* (New York: Replica Books, 1994); Ted A. Smith, *The New Measures: A Theological History of Democratic Practice* (New York: Cambridge University Press, 2007).

[2]Michael J. Wilkins, *Following the Master: Discipleship in the Steps of Jesus* (Grand Rapids: Zondervan, 1992), 31. I am deeply indebted to Mike's scholarship and mentoring for much of my understanding of discipleship in the ancient world. Don't blame Mike for everything you read here, but none of it would have been possible without him. See also Michael J. Wilkins, *The Concept of Disciple in Matthew's Gospel, as Reflected in the Use of the Term "Mathētēs,"* Supplements to Novum Testamentum, vol. 59 (New York: E. J. Brill, 1988); Michael J. Wilkins, *Discipleship in the Ancient World and Matthew's Gospel* (Eugene, OR: Wipf & Stock, 2015); Michael J. Wilkins, *Matthew: From Biblical Text to Contemporary Life*, The NIV Application Commentary (Grand Rapids: Zondervan, 2004).

[3] Like most of our academic programs, the course struggled under pandemic measures and is currently undergoing another rebuild utilizing Dr. Frazier's college-readiness curriculum and this book. See Andrew Martin Frazier, "First-Generation College Students: Making Sense of Academic Advising and Advisor Leadership for Student Success" (EdD diss., University of New England, 2021).

Introduction

[1] There may have been more than fifty books, but I don't want to exaggerate.

[2] I've tweaked names and the precise wording of conversations throughout the book in order to protect students' privacy.

[3] Jesus is quoting from a verse in the Jewish Scriptures, found in Deuteronomy 6:4–5.

[4] Jesus is quoting from another verse in the Jewish Scriptures, found in Leviticus 19:18.

[5] For more on parables, see Joel B. Green, ed., "Parable," in *Dictionary of Jesus and the Gospels* (Downers Grove, IL: InterVarsity Press, 2013), 654–56; and David Stern, *Parables in Midrash: Narrative and Exegesis in Rabbinic Literature* (Cambridge, MA: Harvard University Press, 1991), 93.

[6] Brad H. Young, *The Parables: Jewish Tradition and Christian Interpretation* (Grand Rapids: Baker Academic, 2012), 3.

[7] Jacobus Liebenberg, *The Language of the Kingdom and Jesus*, vol. 102 of *Beihefte Zur Zeitschrift Für Die Neutestamentliche Wissenschaft Und Die Kunde Der Älteren Kirche* (Berlin: Walter de Gruyter, 2001), 68.

[8] Young, *The Parables*, 5.

[9] Donald L. Denton, "Historiography and Hermeneutics in Jesus Studies," *Journal for the Study of the New Testament* 262 (2004): 21.

[10] Or, perhaps more accurately, a *series* of parables.

[11] Since there is currently no universally accepted estimate of Everest's exact height, I will use the highest current estimate of 29,035 feet (8,850 meters). Even if that estimate is a little high, it won't be for long; tectonic pressure causes Everest to grow roughly 16 inches (40 centimeters) per century.

[12] A preternaturally talented climber, George Leigh Mallory eventually rose to the role of "climbing team leader" for the first three British expeditions. The overall expedition leadership charged with getting the team from England to Mount Everest fell to more logistically minded military leaders, such as Lieutenant Colonel Charles Howard-Bury (1921) and Brigadier-General Charles Granville Bruce (1922, 1924).

[13] Mallory established only six of his seven planned expedition camps above base camp. Climbers today often utilize as few as four expedition camps in their acclimatization process. Note: The camp locations in Figure 0.1 are for illustration purposes only and not intended as precise locations. For more literal maps, see Mark Synnott, *The Third Pole: Mystery, Obsession, and Death on Mount Everest* (New York: Dutton, Penguin Random House, 2021), 8–9, 13.

Chapter One: Desire

[1] Peter Gillman and Leni Gillman, *The Wildest Dream: Mallory, His Life, and Conflicting Passions* (London: Headline, 2001), 142.

[2] George Mallory and Peter Gillman, *Climbing Everest: The Complete Writings of George Leigh Mallory* (London: Gibson Square, 2012), 60.

[3] Italics mine. Jon Krakauer, *Into Thin Air: A Personal Account of the Mount Everest Disaster* (New York: Anchor Books, 1999), xvii–xviii.

[4] While the title "rabbi" was likely in use for centuries, the Gospels appear to be the first documents to record the broad use of the term.

[5] Mark 4:38; 9:38; 10:35; Luke 7:40; John 1:38; 11:28; 13:13; 20:16.

[6] Mark 9:17; 10:17, 20; Luke 8:49; 12:13; John 3:2; 8:4.

[7] Matthew 8:19; 9:11; 12:38; 17:24; 19:16; 22:16, 24, 36; Mark 12:14, 32; Luke 10:25; 11:45; 18:18; 19:39; 20:21, 28.

[8] It is unclear how often students learned to read and write in these early schools, but they certainly learned how to memorize and recite.

[9] Martin S. Jaffee, "A Rabbinic Ontology of the Written and Spoken Word: On Discipleship, Transformative Knowledge, and the Living Texts of Oral Torah," *Journal of the American Academy of Religion* 65, no. 3 (1997): 541.

[10] While these three educational tiers probably weren't formalized until the second and third centuries, "By the first century AD many boys were educated in primary and secondary schools." Craig A. Evans and Stanley E. Porter, eds., "Education: Jewish and Greco-Roman," in *Dictionary of New Testament Background* (Downers Grove, IL: InterVarsity Press, 2000), 311–12. See also Fergus Millar, "Empire, Community and Culture in the Roman Near East: Greeks, Syrians, Jews and Arabs," *Journal of Jewish Studies* 38 (1987): 147–48; Christopher A. Rollston, "Scribal Education in Ancient Israel: The Old Hebrew Epigraphic Evidence," *Bulletin of the American Schools of Oriental Research* 344 (Nov. 2006): 47–74; Patrick Pouchelle, "Discipline, Transmission, and Writing: Notes on Education in the Testaments of the Twelve Patriarchs," in *Second Temple Jewish "Paideia" in Context*, ed. Jason M. Zurawski and Gabriele Boccaccini (Berlin: De Gruyter, 2017); Bruce Chilton and Jacob Neusner, *Judaism in the New Testament: Practices and Beliefs* (New York: Routledge, 2006).

[11] Marc G. Hirshman, *The Stabilization of Rabbinic Culture, 100 C.E.–350 C.E.: Texts on Education and their Late Antique Context* (Oxford: Oxford University Press, 2009), 131–32.

[12] Cited in David Bivin, Lois Tverberg, and Bruce Okkema, *New Light on the Difficult Words of Jesus: Insights from His Jewish Context* (Holland, MI: En-Gedi Resource Center, 2007), 12. Yose ben Yoezer, the author of this saying, lived in the first half of the second century BCE and was one of the earliest of the sages of the Mishnah (M. Avot 1:4).

[13] A quote from the tannaitic era (ca. 70–220 CE) cited in Hermann Leberecht Strack and Günter Stemberger, *Introduction to the Talmud and Midrash*, 1st Fortress Press ed. (Minneapolis: Fortress Press, 1992), 4.

[14] Hillel lived from roughly from 110 BCE to 10 CE.

[15] Matthew 9:14; 11:2; 14:12; Mark 2:18; 6:29; Luke 7:18–19; John 1:35; 3:25.

[16] Apparently, John waited forty days while Jesus prayed in the wilderness (Matt. 4:1–13; Mark 1:12–13; Luke 4:1–13).

[17] The other disciple is not named in the text, so most scholars assume he was the Gospel's author, John the Beloved. I will refer to Jesus's student with the name John as "John the Beloved" to avoid confusing him with John the Baptist. It's a fitting title as he refers to himself in the text as "the disciple whom Jesus loved."

[18] Harmonizing the chronology of events in Jesus's life can be tricky, especially when comparing Gospels. Like all ancient historians, the Gospel writers were more interested in organizing their material around various themes than in providing a chronological ordering of events. The slightly different theological purpose and audience of each Gospel often results in chronologies that are difficult to "harmonize." For instance, John's Gospel mentions Jesus's cleansing of the temple as one of the earliest events in Jesus's ministry (John 2:13–16), while Matthew, Mark, and Luke place the cleansing of the temple during the final week of Jesus's life (Matt. 21:12–17; Mark 11:15–19; Luke 19:45–48). Despite these difficulties, a number of scholars have compiled useful (if sometimes wrong-headed) attempts to harmonize the chronology of Jesus's life across the Gospels. They include A. T. Robertson and John Albert Broadus, *A Harmony of the Gospels for Students of the Life of Christ* (New York: Harper & Bros., 1950); and two revisions of Broadus and Robertson's *Harmony* produced by Robert L. Thomas and Stanley N. Gundry: *A Harmony of the Gospels: With Explanations and Essays; Using the Text of the New American Standard Bible* (San Francisco: Harper, 1991); and *The NIV Harmony of the Gospels* (San Francisco: Harper & Row, 1988). A recent addition to this cannon includes Steve Laube, Amanda Jenkins, and Dallas Jenkins, *The Chosen Presents: A Blended Harmony of the Gospels* (Savage, MN: BroadStreet Publishing, 2022). For an ordering less dependent upon conjecture, see Kurt Aland, ed., *Synopsis of the Four Gospels: Completely Revised on the Basis of the Greek Text of the Nestle-Aland 26th Edition and Greek New Testament 3rd Edition; the Text Is the Second Edition of the Revised Standard Version*, rev. printing (New York: American Bible Society, 1982).

[19] Jonathan Edwards, *Religious Affections*, rev. ed., vol. 2 of *The Works of Jonathan Edwards*, gen. ed. Perry Miller (New Haven, CT: Yale University Press, 2009), 96. See also Gerald R. McDermott, *Seeing God: Jonathan Edwards and Spiritual Discernment* (Vancouver, BC: Regent College, 2000); C. Samuel Storms, *Signs of the Spirit: An Interpretation of Jonathan Edwards' Religious Affections* (Wheaton, IL: Crossway Books, 2009); Gary David Stratton, "Review of Jonathan Edwards' Treatise Concerning Religious Affections and Gerald McDermott's *Seeing God*," *Christian Education Journal* 3, no. 1 (Spring 2006): 203–6.

[20] Angela Duckworth, *Grit: The Power of Passion and Perseverance* (New York: Scribner, 2016), 8.

[21] For instance, Matthew, Mark, and Luke (the three *synoptic* Gospels) emphasize how Jesus's disciples began following him as their Teacher, then slowly progressed toward recognizing him as the Messiah somewhere near the midpoint of their discipleship journey. However, in John's Gospel, the disciples *begin* following Jesus as the Messiah so that his Messianic identity motivates their desire to follow him as their Teacher.

Chapter Two: Instruction

[1] Krakauer, *Into Thin Air*, 61.

[2] Here I am following the chronology mapped out by Robertson and Broadus, *A Harmony of the Gospels*, as well as Thomas and Gundry's NIV and NASB chronologies (which do not always agree).

[3] N. T. Wright, *The Challenge of Jesus: Rediscovering Who Jesus Was and Is* (Downers Grove, IL: InterVarsity Press, 1999), 49.

[4] George Mallory, *Climbing Everest: The Complete Writings of George Leigh Mallory*, ed. Peter Gillman (London: Gibson Square, 2012), 108.

[5] Including, but not limited to, the Sermon on the Plain (Luke 6), the parables of the kingdom (Mark 4; Matt. 13), the commissioning of the Twelve (Matt. 10; Mark 3; Luke 9), the commissioning of the seventy (Luke 10), the Olivet Discourse (Matt. 23–25), and the seven discourses of John's Gospel (3:1–36; 4:1–42; 5:19–47; 6:22–66; 7:1–8:59; 10:1–42), including Jesus's Farewell Discourse (John 13–17).

[6] Scot McKnight, *One.Life: Jesus Calls, We Follow* (Grand Rapids: Zondervan, 2010), 31.

[7] Walter Brueggemann, *The Prophetic Imagination*, 40th anniv. ed. (Minneapolis: Fortress Press, 2018), 3.

[8] Matthew uses the phrase "kingdom of *heaven*" where the other Gospel writers use "kingdom of *God*." Scholars suspect he did this to avoid offending his Jewish readers, but Matthew never actually tells us why.

[9] N. T. Wright and Marcus J. Borg, *The Meaning of Jesus: Two Visions* (New York: HarperCollins, 2009), 38.

[10] We will probably have to wait for the reveal in heaven to discover if these are two different sermons, or two separate compilations of Jesus's teaching organized by Matthew and Luke for their respective Gospels' theological purposes.

[11] Daniel Alexander Payne, *Recollections of Seventy Years*, ed. Charles S. Smith (Nashville: Publishing House of the AME Sunday School Union, 1988), 17.

[12] Nelson T. Strobert, *Daniel Alexander Payne: The Venerable Preceptor of the African Methodist Episcopal Church* (Lanham, MD: University Press of America, 2012), 5.

[13] Payne, *Recollections*, 32.

[14] Daniel A. Payne, "Annual Report and Retrospection of Wilberforce University 1873," *Sermons and Addresses, 1853–1891, Religion in America Series* (New York: Arno Press, 1972), 11.

[15] Daniel Alexander Payne, "Wilberforce University," in *Historical Sketches of the Higher Educational Institutions, and Also of Benevolent and Reformatory Institutions of the State of Ohio*, ed. State Commissioner of Common Schools (Columbus: Ohio State Centennial Educational Committee, 1876), 481–82.

[16] The possible exception being AME founder Richard Allen. James T. Campbell, *Songs of Zion: The African Methodist Episcopal Church in the United States and South Africa* (New York: Oxford University Press, 1995), 37.

[17] Klaus Dieter Issler, *Wasting Time with God: A Christian Spirituality of Friendship with God* (Downers Grove, IL: InterVarsity Press, 2001), 102.

[18] It wasn't until much later that I learned they were so automatic because their source was more the fear and trauma stored in my body than my thoughts.

[19] Latin for "I await my protector," which will only make sense if you're a Harry Potter fan, or if you read the story linked to the QR code at the end of Chapter Two.

[20] A great place to start this journey is by reading Steve Cuss, *Managing Leadership Anxiety: Yours and Theirs* (Nashville: Thomas Nelson, 2019).

Chapter Three: Surrender

[1] Krakauer, *Into Thin Air*, 81.

[2] Peter Potterfield, ed., *Everest*, vol. 4 of *The Mountaineers Anthology Series* (Seattle, WA: Mountaineers Books, 2003), 217.

[3] We will return to Jesus's crucial declaration, "This was not revealed to you by flesh and blood, but by my Father in heaven," in Chapter Five: **Intimacy**.

[4] Dave Schmelzer, *Not the Religious Type: Confessions of a Turncoat Atheist* (Carol Stream, IL: SaltRiver, 2008), 37–48.

[5] Eberhard Bethge and Victoria Barnett, *Dietrich Bonhoeffer: Theologian, Christian, Man for His Times; a Biography*, rev. ed (Minneapolis: Fortress Press, 2000), 150–51.

[6] Reggie L. Williams and Ferdinand Schlingensiepen, *Bonhoeffer's Black Jesus: Harlem Renaissance Theology and an Ethic of Resistance*, rev. ed. (Waco, TX: Baylor University Press, 2021), 1.

[7] Bethge and Barnett, *Dietrich Bonhoeffer*, 273–74. Also, Walter Laqueur and Judith Tydor Baumel-Schwartz, eds., *The Holocaust Encyclopedia* (New Haven: Yale University Press, 2001), 496–97.

[8] Bethge and Barnett, *Dietrich Bonhoeffer*, 655.

[9] Dietrich Bonhoeffer, *Dietrich Bonheoffer Works*, vol. 4: *Discipleship*, ed. John D. Godsey and Geffrey B. Kelly (Minneapolis: Fortress Press, 2003), 44–45.

[10] Lee C. Camp, *Mere Discipleship: Radical Christianity in a Rebellious World*, 2nd ed. (Grand Rapids: Brazos Press, 2008), 105.

[11] Cuss, *Managing Leadership Anxiety*, 20.

¹²Peter Scazzero, *Emotionally Healthy Discipleship: Moving from Shallow Christianity to Deep Transformation* (Grand Rapids: Zondervan, 2021).

Chapter Four: Community

¹Who fed all of Israel with bread from heaven in the wilderness (Exod. 16).

²Lyon viewed being passed off to her older brother's care as the economic necessity of a woman struggling to raise seven children rather than a personal betrayal and remained close to her mother for life.

³Fidelia Fisk, *Recollections of Mary Lyon: With Selections from Her Instructions to the Pupils in Mt. Holyoke Female Seminary* (Boston, MA: American Tract Society, 1866), 30.

⁴Fisk, *Recollections of Mary Lyon*, 37.

⁵Edward Hitchcock, *The Power of Christian Benevolence Illustrated in the Life and Labors of Mary Lyon* (New York: American Tract Society, 1858), 20.

⁶Fisk, *Recollections of Mary Lyon*, 37.

⁷Jewel A. Smith, *Transforming Women's Education: Liberal Arts and Music in Female Seminaries* (Urbana: University of Illinois Press, 2019), 49.

⁸Smith, *Transforming Women's Education*, 49.

⁹Michael James McClymond, ed., *Encyclopedia of Religious Revivals in America* (Westport, CT: Greenwood Press, 2007), xv–xxi.

¹⁰Michael James McClymond and Gerald R. McDermott, *The Theology of Jonathan Edwards* (New York: Oxford University Press, 2012), 21.

¹¹Amanda Porterfield, *Mary Lyon and the Mount Holyoke Missionaries* (New York: Oxford University Press, 1997), 17.

¹²Acts 9:26–30; 11:19–26.

¹³Roughly $50,000 in 2023 buying power.

¹⁴Porterfield, *Mary Lyon*, 11.

¹⁵Joseph Conforti, "Mary Lyon, the Founding of Mount Holyoke College, and the Cultural Revival of Jonathan Edwards," *Religion and American Culture: A Journal of Interpretation* 3, no. 1 (1993): 75.

¹⁶Porterfield, *Mary Lyon*, 6.

¹⁷Porterfield, *Mary Lyon*, 6.

¹⁸Dana Lee Robert, *American Women in Mission: A Social History of Their Thought and Practice* (Macon, GA: Mercer University Press, 1996), 259.

¹⁹Gary David Stratton, "Northfield Conference (1886–1899)," in *The Encyclopedia of Christianity in the United States*, ed. George Thomas Kurian and Mark A. Lamport (Lanham, MD: Rowman and Littlefield, 2016), 1648.

²⁰Fisk, *Recollections of Mary Lyon*, 99.

²¹Porterfield, *Mary Lyon*, 4.

²²Fisk, *Recollections of Mary Lyon*, 53.

²³See Acts 2:42–48 for how this Table fellowship transformed the disciples of Jesus's disciples.

²⁴Henri J. M. Nouwen, "Moving from Solitude to Community to Ministry," *Leadership Journal* 16, no. 2 (Spring 1995): 67—italics mine.

[25]Note: Forgiveness does not automatically imply trust, especially when the wounding is deep, persistent, and/or secretive. Unscrupulous "Christians" sometimes seek to exploit a healthy community's or individuals' willingness to forgive by demanding continued trust. But while forgiveness is unconditional, trust is earned. If you believe someone is seeking to take advantage of your willingness to forgive, seek immediate help from a licensed counselor or spiritual leader from outside the community.

Chapter Five: Intimacy

[1]The 1921 expedition actually brought bottles of medical oxygen with them, but after the death of their oxygen expert, Dr. Alexander Kellas, they never attempted to use them for climbing.

[2]Edward Felix Norton, *The Fight for Everest 1924* (Sheffield: Edward Arnold & Co., 1925), 222.

[3]Until the discovery of Mallory's body, most assumed the climbing partners fell on their way up. However, the 1999 expedition uncovered indirect evidence to the contrary in Mallory's well-preserved climbing jacket. First, Mallory's sunglasses were in his pocket. Since snow blindness results from climbers failing to wear their sunglasses during the day, one can only assume Mallory was alive until late in the day or even night. That's when he would have put them in his pocket. This leaves more than enough time for the climbers to have reached the summit and returned to the cliffs above where Mallory's body was found.

Even more intriguing, two missing items in Mallory's climbing jacket also point to the possibility of a successful summit. While letters from Ruth and friends remained wrapped in a handkerchief in Mallory's pocket, the photo of Ruth he planned to leave on the summit was missing. So was his camera, which he presumably would have handed to Irvine to snap a mountaintop photo.

Lacking any objective proof, few credit Mallory and Irvine with Everest's first summit—a feat no mountaineer would accomplish for another thirty years. However, the hunt for Irvine's body and the missing camera continues and may yet provide further evidence for or against a successful summit in 1924. For a great read concerning the search for Irvine's body and Mallory's camera, see Mark Synnott, *The Third Pole: Mystery, Obsession, and Death on Mount Everest* (New York: Dutton, 2021).

[4]Notable exceptions include a few extraordinary individuals, such as Reinhold Messner and Peter Habeler, who proved in 1978 that it is possible to summit Everest without supplemental oxygen.

[5]See Todd W. Hall and M. Elizabeth Lewis Hall, *Relational Spirituality: A Psychological-Theological Paradigm for Transformation* (Downers Grove, IL: InterVarsity Press, 2021), 97–137.

[6]Jonathan Edwards, "A Divine and Supernatural Light (Matt. 16:17)," in *Sermons and Discourses, 1730–1733*, ed. Mark R. Valeri, vol. 17 of *The Works of Jonathan Edwards* (New Haven, CT: Yale University Press, 1999), 405–27.

[7] J. I. Packer, *Knowing God* (Downers Grove, IL: InterVarsity Press, 2021).

[8] Edwards, "A Divine and Supernatural Light," 407.

[9] J. Scott Duvall and J. Daniel Hays, *God's Relational Presence: The Cohesive Center of Biblical Theology* (Grand Rapids: Baker Academic, 2019), 181.

[10] In full disclosure, the Greek grammar could also read, "We have come to believe and to know," rather than, "We believe and have come to know." However, either translation supports the assertion that belief and knowledge grow over time due to God's revelation. Likely, the disciples' belief/knowledge began in their human ("flesh and blood") understanding and grew into divinely revealed experiential knowledge.

[11] Ruth H. Barton, *Sacred Rhythms: Arranging Our Lives for Spiritual Transformation* (Downers Grove, IL: InterVarsity Press, 2006), 12.

[12] James D. G. Dunn, *The Evidence for Jesus* (Philadelphia: The Westminster Press, 1985), 48.

[13] Simon Chan, *Spiritual Theology: A Systematic Study of the Christian Life* (Downers Grove, IL: InterVarsity Press, 1998), 132.

[14] Teresa of Ávila, *The Interior Castle*, trans. Mirabai Starr (New York: Riverhead Books, 2004), 6.

[15] Sometimes called "the Prayer of Quiet."

[16] Brother Lawrence, *The Practice of the Presence of God*, trans. John J. Delaney (Garden City, NY: Image Books, 1977), 27.

[17] John of the Cross, *Dark Night of the Soul* (Boston: Wyatt North Publishing, 2012). John was a mentee of Teresa of Ávila.

[18] C. S. Lewis, *The Screwtape Letters: Also Includes "Screwtape Proposes a Toast"* (New York: Touchstone, 1996), 42.

[19] C. S. Lewis, *The Lion, the Witch, and the Wardrobe*, book 1 of *The Chronicles of Narnia* (1950; reprint, New York: HarperCollins, 1994), 163.

[20] Cynthia Bourgeault, *Centering Prayer and Inner Awakening* (Cambridge, MA: Cowley Publications, 2004), 24.

Chapter Six: Prayer

[1] Ed Caesar, *The Moth and the Mountain: A True Story of Love, War, and Everest* (New York: Avid Reader Press, 2020), 214.

[2] Caesar, *The Moth and the Mountain*, 109.

[3] Caesar, *The Moth and the Mountain*, 170.

[4] Caesar, *The Moth and the Mountain*, 214.

[5] In Jewish idiom, Jesus's words likely sounded more chiding than angry— something like your exasperated grandmother or Billy Crystal's Miracle Max in *The Princess Bride*.

[6] Many early manuscripts do not include the phrase "and fasting."

[7] Once again, Gospel chronologies can be tricky, but all three synoptics place the failure of the nine disciples to help the demon-afflicted boy *after* Jesus granted them authority over demons. Luke even sets their commission

immediately beforehand. See Matthew 10:1; 17:14–21; Mark 6:7; 9:14–29; Luke 9:1, 37–43.

[8] Luke 3:21; 5:16; 6:12; 9:18, 28; 10:17–21; 11:1; 22:39–46; 23:34, 46.

[9] James D. G. Dunn, *Pneumatology*, vol. 2 of *The Christ and the Spirit: Collected Essays of James D. G. Dunn* (Grand Rapids: Eerdmans, 1998), 137–38.

[10] Marianne Meye Thompson, *The Promise of the Father: Jesus and God in the New Testament* (Louisville, KY: Westminster John Knox Press, 2000), 73–75.

[11] David F. Wells, "Prayer: Rebelling against the Status Quo; Are We Angry Enough to Pray?," *Christianity Today* 23, no. 25 (Nov. 2, 1979): 37.

[12] This is the meta-story behind much of the New Testament. Jesus taught his students that, through his journey to the cross, "the prince of this world will be driven out" so he can "draw all people to [him]self" (John 12:31–32). John the Beloved later writes, "The reason the Son of God appeared was to destroy the devil's work" (1 John 3:8). Peter explains, "How God anointed Jesus of Nazareth with the Holy Spirit and power, and how he went around doing good and healing all who were under the power of the devil, because God was with him" (Acts 10:38). The apostle Paul tells us that Jesus's obedience "disarmed the powers and authorities, [and] made a public spectacle of them, triumphing over them by the cross" (Col. 2:15), so that now, "He has rescued us from the dominion of darkness and brought us into the kingdom of the Son he loves" (Col. 1:13).

[13] *Stranger Things*, season 1, episode 5, "The Flea and the Acrobat," directed by Matt Duffer and Ross Duffer, written by Matt Duffer, Ross Duffer, and Alison Tatlock, featuring Winona Ryder, David Harbour, and Finn Wolfhard, Netflix, aired July 15, 2016.

[14] For which Gary Oldman won the Academy Award for Best Actor. See Joe Wright, dir., *Darkest Hour*, Universal Pictures Home Entertainment, 2018; Christopher Nolan, dir., *Dunkirk*, Warner Bros. Home Entertainment, 2017.

[15] Norman Grubb, *Rees Howells, Intercessor: The Story of a Life Lived for God* (London: CLC Publications, 2016), 166–72. See also Doris Ruscoe, *The Intercession of Rees Howells* (Cambridge, UK: Lutterworth Press, 2003).

[16] Nevile Henderson, *Failure of a Mission: Berlin 1937–1939* (New York: G. P. Putnam's Sons, 1940), 95.

[17] Peter Ross Range, *1924: The Year That Made Hitler* (New York: Little, Brown and Company, 2016), 107.

[18] Raymond E. Brown, *The Community of the Beloved Disciple*, vol. 2 (New York: Paulist Press, 1979), 662–63.

[19] It is hard to miss the parallel to James 4:2–3, "You do not have because you do not ask God. When you ask, you do not receive, because you ask with wrong motives, that you may spend what you get on your pleasures."

[20] Craig S. Keener, *The Gospel of John: A Commentary*, vol. 2 (Peabody, MA: Hendrickson Publishers, 2003), 998.

[21] Richard J. Foster, *Prayer: Finding the Heart's True Home* (San Francisco: Harper, 1992), 3.

[22] Due to the prevalence of eating disorders, I strongly recommend students never skip more than one meal per week on their own, and that any group who decides to fast longer than one meal should seek the guidance of a trusted faculty or staff member, and/or their pastor.

[23] For the record, I do not recommend students fast for seven days in the middle of a busy term.

Chapter Seven: Love

[1] Assuming Mallory and Irvine failed in 1924.

[2] Miranda Lin-Manuel and Jeremy McCarter, *Hamilton: The Revolution; Being the Complete Libretto of the Broadway Musical with a True Account of Its Creation and Concise Remarks on Hip-Hop, the Power of Stories, and the New America*, 1st ed. (New York: Grand Central Publishing, 2016).

[3] John was also one of only three students invited to the "garden where it happens" when Jesus requested prayer support in Gethsemane (Mark 14:32–42). Later that night, John's family connections got him (and Peter) into "the house where it happens" when Jesus appeared before the high priest Caiaphas (although Peter probably wished he had stayed outside). As far as we know, John was the only one of the Twelve who made it to "the hill where it happened" when Jesus was crucified (John 13:18–30).

[4] Matthew 26:31–35; Mark 9:34; 14:27–31; Luke 9:46–48; 22:24–38; John 13:31–38.

[5] Mark emphasizes the carte blanche nature of their family request: "Teacher, we want you to do for us *whatever* we ask" (Mark 10:36—italics mine).

[6] Here again, I am following the chronology of Robertson, Thomas, and Gundry.

[7] James K. A. Smith, *You Are What You Love: The Spiritual Power of Habit* (Grand Rapids: Brazos Press, 2016), 2.

[8] Tertullian, *The Apologetic Writings: Excerpted from the Ante-Nicene Fathers* (n.p.: Veritatis Splendor Publications, 2012), 145.

[9] Eusebius, *Collected Works of Eusebius*, trans. Andrew Smith (East Sussex: Delphi Classics, 2019).

[10] Martin Luther King Jr., "Nonviolence: The Only Road to Freedom," in *A Testament of Hope: The Essential Writings and Speeches of Martin Luther King, Jr*, ed. James Melvin Washington (San Francisco: Harper, 1991), 54–61.

[11] Martin Luther King Jr., "'The Role of the Church in Facing the Nation's Chief Moral Dilemma': Address Delivered on 25 April 1957 at the Conference on Christian Faith and Human Relations in Nashville," Stanford University, https://kinginstitute.stanford.edu/king-papers/documents/role-church-facing-nation-s-chief-moral-dilemma-address-delivered-25-april.

[12] Robert Chao Romero, "Faith and Race," Council for Christian Colleges and Universities, 2021.

[13] John 13:23; 19:26; 20:2; 21:7, 20.

[14] Henri J. M. Nouwen, "Moving from Solitude to Community to Ministry," *Leadership Journal* 16, no. 2 (Spring 1995): 66.

[15] David G. Benner, *I Am the Love That Flows through Me* (Ontario: Cascadia Living Wisdom Publishing, 2022), 105–6.

[16] Michael H. Kibbe, "Light That Conquers the Darkness: Oscar Romero on the Transfiguration of Jesus," *Theology Today* 75, no. 4 (Jan. 2019): 447.

[17] Kevin Michael Clarke, *Oscar Romero: Love Must Win Out* (Collegeville, MN: Liturgical Press, 2014), 39.

[18] Julio O. Torres, *Oscar Romero: A Man for Our Times* (New York: Seabury Books, 2021), 31–32, 68, 70.

[19] Robert Chao Romero, *Brown Church: Five Centuries of Latina/o Social Justice, Theology, and Identity* (Downers Grove, IL: InterVarsity Press, 2020), 167.

[20] Oscar A. Romero, *The Scandal of Redemption: When God Liberates the Poor, Saves Sinners, and Heals Nations*, ed. Carolyn Kurtz (Walden, NY: Plough Publishing House, 2018), 6.

[21] Kibbe, "Light That Conquers," 447.

[22] Torres, *Man for Our Times*, 87.

[23] O. Romero, *Scandal of Redemption*, 7–8.

[24] R. Romero, *Brown Church*, 145—italics mine.

[25] O. Romero, *Scandal of Redemption*, 73, 9–10, 73.

[26] James R. Brockman, *Romero: A Life* (Maryknoll, NY: Orbis Books, 2005), 36.

[27] Torres, *Man for Our Times*, 88.

[28] O. Romero, *Scandal of Redemption*, 73.

[29] Marie Dennis, Renny Golden, and Scott Wright, *Oscar Romero: Reflections on His Life and Writings* (Maryknoll, NY: Orbis Books, 2000), 105.

[30] "The lynching tree—so strikingly similar to the cross on Golgotha—should have a prominent place in American images of Jesus' death. But it does not." James H. Cone, *The Cross and the Lynching Tree* (Maryknoll, NY: Orbis Books, 2011), 42.

[31] "The closest parallel to the modern police were the soldiers tasked with the work of keeping order in the cities and towns of the empire." Esau McCaulley, *Reading While Black: African American Biblical Interpretation as an Exercise in Hope* (Downers Grove, IL: InterVarsity Press, 2020), 45.

[32] Sandra Uwiringiyimana, *How Dare the Sun Rise: Memoirs of a War Child* (New York: Katherine Tegen Books, 2017), 6.

Chapter Eight: Embodiment

[1] Sherpa place their surnames before their first names, so Tenzing Norgay is referred to as "Tenzing," while Edmund Hillary is referred to as "Hillary."

[2] She also knighted the expedition leader, John Hunt.

[3] The controversy centered on an international debate as to whether Tenzing Norgay was Nepali, and therefore a Chinese citizen, or Indian, and therefore a British citizen. Fearing any offense to Mao Zedong's newly established communist government, the queen's officials declined knighting Tenzing,

despite the fact that he had lived in India for decades. Seventy years after their summit, Britain's snub of Everest's "invisible man" continues to stir contention.

⁴Hillary never changed their story, even after Tenzing's 1955 biography claimed Hillary made the final step to the summit a moment before him. Many believe Tenzing was paid a large sum of money to go along with this fib.

⁵Matthew 27:33; Mark 15:22; Luke 23:33; John 19:17.

⁶Luke 22:39–46; Matthew 26:36–46; Mark 14:32–42.

⁷John 20:17; Luke 24:26, 46; Matthew 28:18.

⁸All this despite the unfair and often discriminatory working conditions facing the Sherpa. It is not uncommon for Everest guiding firms to pay Sherpa less than $5,000 for working the entire two-month climbing season, while charging $50,000 to $100,000 per climber to get their rich clients to the top of Everest. Sherpa do all the hard work of setting up camps and placing guide ropes, while taking the greatest risks. Sherpa account for nearly 40 percent of all Everest deaths, including twenty-three Sherpa who perished in avalanches in 2014 and 2015 alone.

⁹Jacob Neusner, *The Four Stages of Rabbinic Judaism* (New York: Routledge, 1999), viii.

¹⁰Cited in Bruce Chilton and Jacob Neusner, "Paul and Gamaliel," *Review of Rabbinic Judaism* 8, no. 1–2 (2005): 46.

¹¹Martin S. Jaffee, "A Rabbinic Ontology of the Written and Spoken Word: On Discipleship, Transformative Knowledge, and the Living Texts of Oral Torah," *Journal of the American Academy of Religion* 65, no. 3 (1997): 541.

¹²Note: Osborn only narrowly avoided the wrath of the masters of the slaves she taught by organizing them into meetings where they would be separated from White community members. Such was the world of eighteenth-century Rhode Island.

¹³Sarah Osborn, *Sarah Osborn's Collected Writings*, ed. Catherine A. Brekus (New Haven, CT: Yale University Press, 2017), 313.

¹⁴Samuel Hopkins, *A Dialogue Concerning Slavery of the Africans, Showing It to Be the Duty and Interest of the American States to Emancipate All Their African Slaves*, ed. Peter Force (New York: Judah P. Spooner, 1776; reprinted for Robert Hodge, 1785).

¹⁵Samuel Hopkins, *Memoirs of the Life of Mrs. Sarah Osborn: Who Died in Newport, on the Second Day of August, 1796, in the Eighty-Third Year of Her Age* (Gale & Sabin International, 2012).

¹⁶Gardiner Spring, "Christian Sanctification," in *The Literary and Theological Review* (New York: Appleton, 1834), 1: 115.

¹⁷Charles Grier Sellers, *The Market Revolution: Jacksonian America 1815–1846* (New York: Oxford University Press, 1994), 206.

¹⁸Joseph L. Locke and Ben Wright, eds., *The American Yawp: A Massively Collaborative Open U.S. History Textbook* (Stanford: Stanford University Press, 2019), 271.

[19] Amy L. Sherman, *Kingdom Calling: Vocational Stewardship for the Common Good* (Downers Grove, IL: InterVarsity Press, 2011), 100.

[20] Dallas Willard, *The Great Omission: Reclaiming Jesus's Essential Teachings on Discipleship* (San Francisco: HarperOne, 2006), xv.

[21] N. T. Wright, *The Challenge of Jesus: Rediscovering Who Jesus Was and Is* (Downers Grove, IL: InterVarsity Press, 1999), 196.

[22] *Braveheart*, directed by Mel Gibson, written by Randall Wallace, featuring Mel Gibson, Brendan Gleeson, Patrick McGoohan, and Sophie Marceau (Los Angeles: Paramount Pictures, 1995).

[23] Including other films such as *Secretariat, Pearl Harbor, We Were Soldiers*, and *Heaven Is for Real*.

[24] Frederick Buechner, *Wishful Thinking: A Seeker's ABC*, rev. and expanded ed. (San Francisco: Harper, 1993).

[25] Parker J. Palmer, *Let Your Life Speak: Listening for the Voice of Vocation* (San Francisco: Jossey-Bass, 2000), 6.

[26] Howard Thurman, *The Living Wisdom of Howard Thurman: A Visionary for Our Time* (Louisville, KY: Sounds True, 2011), audio recordings.

Epilogue

[1] Lene Gammelgaard, *Climbing High: A Woman's Account of Surviving the Everest Tragedy* (New York: HarperPerennial, 2000), 23.

[2] Gammelgaard, *Climbing High*, 173–74.

[3] Junko Tabei and Helen Y. Rolfe, *Honouring High Places: The Mountain Life of Junko Tabei*, trans. Yumiko Hiraki and Rieko Holtved (Victoria, BC: RMB, 2017), 12.

[4] *Creed*, dir. Ryan Coogler, written by Ryan Coogler, Aaron Covington, and Sylvester Stallone, featuring Michael B. Jordan, Sylvester Stallone, and Tessa Thompson (Burbank, CA: Warner Bros. Entertainment, 2015).

[5] John Calvin, *Institutes of the Christian Religion*, ed. John T. McNeill (Lousiville, KY: Westminster John Knox, 1960), 1034.

[6] As a young Jesus follower, I permanently memorized this verse from reciting it to myself multiple times each day.

[7] John Wesley, *A Plain Account of Christian Perfection*, ed. Randy L. Maddox and Paul W. Chilcote (Kansas City, MO: Beacon Hill, 2015), 13.